# Practical XMPP

Unleash the power of XMPP in order to build exciting, real-time, federated applications based on open standards in a secure and highly scalable fashion

**Lloyd Watkin**
**David Koelle**

[PACKT] open source*
PUBLISHING     community experience distilled

BIRMINGHAM - MUMBAI

# Practical XMPP

First published: September 2016

Production reference: 1280916

Published by Packt Publishing Ltd.
Livery Place
35 Livery Street
Birmingham
B3 2PB, UK.
ISBN 978-1-78528-798-5

www.packtpub.com

# Credits

**Authors**

Lloyd Watkin

David Koelle

**Reviewers**

Emilien Kenler

Ian Wild

**Commissioning Editor**

Edward Gordon

**Acquisition Editor**

Reshma Raman

**Content Development Editor**

Mayur Pawanikar

**Technical Editor**

Karan Thakkar

**Copy Editors**

Vikrant Phadke

Safis Editing

**Project Coordinator**

Nidhi Joshi

**Proofreader**

Safis Editing

**Indexer**

Aishwarya Gangawane

**Production Coordinator**

Arvindkumar Gupta

# About the Authors

**Lloyd Watkin** has over 10 years of experience in building for the Web. A great believer in open source and open standards, he has contributed to, started, and led many successful open source projects and is also an international conference speaker.

Lloyd was knowingly introduced to XMPP in 2012 and hasn't looked back. Its open standard base and the ability to code clients, servers, components in any language leads to a very diverse and healthy environment. Its relevance only seems to increase as new technologies (not imagined at the time of creation) come into existence.

> *I would like to thank my family and friends for their support and damaged ear drums. I would also like to thank the XSF and the XMPP community as a whole for being supportive, welcoming, and always striving to improve and extend the XMPP ecosystem.*

**David Koelle** is a principal software engineer at Charles River Analytics Inc. in Cambridge, Massachusetts, USA, where he has employed XMPP on projects to facilitate collaboration and shared situational awareness among distant teams. He is also the author of JFugue, a popular open source music programming API for Java and other JVM languages, and he is a co-organizer for the Boston Android Meetup.

David has delivered several award-winning talks at high-profile conferences including JavaOne and SXSW. In addition to his technical work in software engineering and systems engineering, he finds opportunities to mentor engineers to help them grow in their careers and recognize the value that proactive leadership can bring to engineers and their environments. David is a graduate of Worcester Polytechnic Institute (WPI).

# About the Reviewers

**Emilien Kenler**, after working on small web projects, began focusing on game development in 2008 while he was in high school. Until 2011, he worked for different groups and specialized in system administration.

In 2011, he founded a company that sold Minecraft servers while studying Computer Science Engineering. He created a lightweight IaaS (`https://github.com/HostYourCreeper/`) based on new technologies such as Node.js and RabbitMQ.

Thereafter, he worked at TaDaweb as a system administrator, building its infrastructure and creating tools to manage deployments and monitoring.

In 2014, he began a new adventure at Wizcorp, Tokyo. The same year, Emilien graduated from the University of Technology of Compiègne, France.

Since 2016, he's a systems engineer at Vesper, the company behind TableSolution, a leading restaurant reservation and CRM system.

Emilien has written *MariaDB Essentials, Packt Publishing*. He has also contributed as a reviewer on *Learning Nagios 4, MariaDB High Performance, OpenVZ Essentials, Vagrant Virtual Development Environment Cookbook, Getting Started with MariaDB Second Edition* and *Mastering Redis*, all by Packt Publishing.

**Ian Wild's** career has always focused primarily on communication and learning. Ian, a physicist by profession, spent 15 years in private industry designing communication systems software (Lucent Technologies, Avaya) before specializing in the development and deployment of learning management systems. Ian has a particular interest in the integration of legacy systems. He is currently the lead developer for Skills for Health, the sector skills council for the UK's health sector. He is responsible for one of the country's busiest online learning platforms (the National Skills Academy for Health).

# www.PacktPub.com

## eBooks, discount offers, and more

Did you know that Packt offers eBook versions of every book published, with PDF and ePub files available? You can upgrade to the eBook version at www.PacktPub.com and as a print book customer, you are entitled to a discount on the eBook copy. Get in touch with us at customercare@packtpub.com for more details.

At www.PacktPub.com, you can also read a collection of free technical articles, sign up for a range of free newsletters and receive exclusive discounts and offers on Packt books and eBooks.

https://www2.packtpub.com/books/subscription/packtlib

Do you need instant solutions to your IT questions? PacktLib is Packt's online digital book library. Here, you can search, access, and read Packt's entire library of books.

## Why subscribe?

- Fully searchable across every book published by Packt
- Copy and paste, print, and bookmark content
- On demand and accessible via a web browser

# Table of Contents

# Preface

XMPP has been around since 1999, and in that time has been rediscovered several times over by generation after generation of programmers. Originally started to unify what was a massively fragmented instant messaging scene, XMPP has continued to show its relevance as new technologies and technology uses emerge.

We'll be making use of the Prosody XMPP server, a fast, resource light system written in LUA, as well as Node.js to write our own projects. The two main libraries we'll be using to interact with XMPP are node-xmpp on the server side and XMPP-FTW, a translation layer between XMPP's XML messages and JSON, which is massively popular for use in the browser.

Through this book, you'll learn about the core concepts of XMPP, build basic clients that will allow you to interact with the XMPP ecosystem at large, build time-saving bots, and even build an entire custom application using XMPP standards and your own extensions.

The skills you'll learn in this book will allow you to create the next massively popular chat application built on the core standards, through to your own full-fledged Internet of Things (IoT) device that will collect, share, and respond to data from interconnected servers all over the world!

## What this book covers

Chapter 1, *An Introduction to XMPP and Installing Our First Server*. Provides a brief introduction to the history of XMPP and its uses as well as installing and interacting with our first XMPP server.

Chapter 2, *Diving into the Core XMPP Concepts, reveals that* XMPP covers a vast number of areas but at its core is very simple and extensible. Here we learn about the core concepts so when we come to building our XMPP applications later we understand what's going on.

Chapter 3, *Building a One-on-One Chat Bot - The "Hello World" of XMPP*, show us how to build a simple chat bot and interact with it via a standard client.

Chapter 4, *Talking XMPP in the Browser Using XMPP-FTW*, we introduce XMPP-FTW and shows us how to build some basic functionality.

Chapter 5, *Building a Multi-User Chat Application*, how to create a very basic multi user chat client in the browser and begin chatting with our XMPP users.

Chapter 6, *Make Your Static Website Real-Time*, takes a standard static website and add real time data to it pushed via XMPP, making even the dullest website dynamic and exciting!

Chapter 7, *Creating an XMPP Component*, shows how to create our first server-side component, which let you develop business logic without modifying the server itself.

Chapter 8, *Building a Basic XMPP-Based Pong Game*, how to create a simple application, using standard chat messages to convey game state. We also learn about Client DISCO for discovering capabilities of a client connected to a chat server.

Chapter 9, *Enhancing XMPPong with a Server Component and Custom Messages*, explains *how to* develop a full-fledged XMPP demonstration application, including a server-side component, an XMPP-FTW extension that allows us to create our own messages, and clients that talk to the server using those messages.

Chapter 10, *Real-World Deployment and XMPP Extensions*, presents considerations for deploying your app, including security and scalability. These capabilities are described in XMPP Extension Protocols (XEPs), and in this chapter we also take the opportunity to introduce several additional XEPs that describe emerging XMPP features, including Internet of Things and WebRTC.

# What you need for this book

The requirements for all sections of this book after fairly minimal. Any computer built within the past five years that supports a recent version of Linux, Mac, or Windows will be sufficient. An up-to-date browser will be required for websocket support, but even then the project is able to fall back to standard HTTP. You machine should have at least 128 Mb of free RAM and the same amount of hard drive space.

# Who this book is for

If you want to learn about the fundamentals of XMPP, be able to work with the core functionality both server-side and in the browser, then this book is for you. No knowledge of XMPP is required, or of TCP/IP networking. It's important that you already know how to build applications of some form, and are looking get a better understanding of how to implement XMPP for one or more of its many uses. You should be interested in the decentralized web, know HTML, and know JavaScript and NodeJS. You will probably know JSON, and hopefully XML (this is the native output of XMPP).

# Conventions

In this book, you will find a number of text styles that distinguish between different kinds of information. Here are some examples of these styles and an explanation of their meaning.

Code words in text, database table names, folder names, filenames, file extensions, pathnames, dummy URLs, user input, and Twitter handles are shown as follows: First we'll install `libicu` and `libexpat-dev`.

A block of code is set as follows:

```
modules_enabled = {
        "roster";
        "saslauth";
        "tls";
        "dialback";
        "disco";
        "version";
        "uptime";
        "time";
        "ping",
        "register";
        "posix";
        "bosh";
};
```

Any command-line input or output is written as follows:

```
$ curl https://raw.githubusercontent.com/creationix/nvm/v0.32.0/install.sh
| bash
$ source ~/.bashrc
$ nvm install 6
$ node -v
```

**New terms** and **Important words** are shown in bold. Words that you see on the screen, for example, in menus or dialog boxes, appear in the text like this: "The shortcuts in this book are based on the Mac OS X 10.5+ scheme."

Warnings or important notes appear in a box like this.

Tips and tricks appear like this.

# Reader feedback

Feedback from our readers is always welcome. Let us know what you think about this book-what you liked or disliked. Reader feedback is important for us as it helps us develop titles that you will really get the most out of. To send us general feedback, simply e-mail feedback@packtpub.com, and mention the book's title in the subject of your message. If there is a topic that you have expertise in and you are interested in either writing or contributing to a book, see our author guide at www.packtpub.com/authors.

# Customer support

Now that you are the proud owner of a Packt book, we have a number of things to help you to get the most from your purchase.

# Downloading the example code

You can download the example code files for this book from your account at http://www.packtpub.com. If you purchased this book elsewhere, you can visit http://www.packtpub.com/support and register to have the files e-mailed directly to you.

You can download the code files by following these steps:

1. Log in or register to our website using your e-mail address and password.
2. Hover the mouse pointer on the **SUPPORT** tab at the top.
3. Click on **Code Downloads & Errata**.
4. Enter the name of the book in the **Search** box.
5. Select the book for which you're looking to download the code files.
6. Choose from the drop-down menu where you purchased this book from.
7. Click on **Code Download**.

Once the file is downloaded, please make sure that you unzip or extract the folder using the latest version of:

- WinRAR / 7-Zip for Windows
- Zipeg / iZip / UnRarX for Mac
- 7-Zip / PeaZip for Linux

The code bundle for the book is also hosted on GitHub at `https://github.com/PacktPubl ishing/Practical-XMPP`. We also have other code bundles from our rich catalog of books and videos available at `https://github.com/PacktPublishing/`. Check them out!

# Errata

Although we have taken every care to ensure the accuracy of our content, mistakes do happen. If you find a mistake in one of our books-maybe a mistake in the text or the code-we would be grateful if you could report this to us. By doing so, you can save other readers from frustration and help us improve subsequent versions of this book. If you find any errata, please report them by visiting `http://www.packtpub.com/submit-errata`, selecting your book, clicking on the **Errata Submission Form** link, and entering the details of your errata. Once your errata are verified, your submission will be accepted and the errata will be uploaded to our website or added to any list of existing errata under the Errata section of that title.

To view the previously submitted errata, go to `https://www.packtpub.com/books/conten t/support` and enter the name of the book in the search field. The required information will appear under the **Errata** section.

# Piracy

Piracy of copyrighted material on the Internet is an ongoing problem across all media. At Packt, we take the protection of our copyright and licenses very seriously. If you come across any illegal copies of our works in any form on the Internet, please provide us with the location address or website name immediately so that we can pursue a remedy.

Please contact us at `copyright@packtpub.com` with a link to the suspected pirated material.

We appreciate your help in protecting our authors and our ability to bring you valuable content.

# Questions

If you have a problem with any aspect of this book, you can contact us at `questions@packtpub.com`, and we will do our best to address the problem.

# 1
# An Introduction to XMPP and Installing Our First Server

Picture this scene: It's 1999 and you have just received your brand new computer, which sports a super-fast 333 MHz processor, a massive 256 MB of RAM, and a copy of the latest operating system, Windows 98. Not only that, but it also has a 33.6 kbps modem. After setting a wallpaper of your favorite mountain range and adjusting the screensaver to have a cool floating 3D effect, you set about connecting yourself to the information superhighway.

Soon, colleagues and friends find out that you have got yourself connected and start inviting you to connect. Jennifer in the office is using ICQ, so you also install ICQ and start chatting. Meanwhile, you've received an e-mail from your friend Marty, who asks you to install AOL Instant Messenger. Not wanting to be left out, you sign up and connect there too. Several weeks later, you've also installed Yahoo! Instant Messenger and MSN Messenger.

Now, each time your modem completes making the bing-bong electronic noises, you instinctively fire up several instant messaging applications to ensure you don't miss any messages from friends, family, and colleagues. Worse still, if you want to have a group chat with Linda and Marvin, that's not possible since both of your friends have decided to use different instant messaging programs. You begin to think to yourself that there has to be a better way.

Enter XMPP, a federated secure set of standards that allow clients and servers to talk to each other in a common language.

In this chapter, we'll cover the following topics:

- What is XMPP?
- Uses of XMPP
- XMPP and the Web
- Installing Node.js
- Installing, configuring, and testing our XMPP server
- Creating a test account and connecting

# What is XMPP?

Work on a new instant messaging system designed to solve the aforementioned problems began in 1998 with the development of the **Extensible Messaging and Presence Protocol**, or **XMPP**, and the first XMPP server was made available by January 1999.

Over the next 6 years, the **Jabber** software and standards were defined and eventually approved by the **Internet Engineering Task Force** (**IETF**). Jabber became known as XMPP during that process. The process of becoming part of the IETF meant that the protocol underwent a huge amount of scrutiny, laying the foundations for the maturity and security in the protocol that we are seeing today.

Additional standards were created later that extended the platform so that it could handle things such as voice and video calls, Multi-User Chat (MUC), publish-subscribe systems, avatars, vCards, and feature discovery. These standards are looked after by a body called the XMPP Standards Foundation, or XSF, which handles the publishing, editing, finalizing, and obsoleting of the standards.

The important thing to realize about XMPP is that rather than being a set of software, it is a set of standards that define how clients and servers should interact, much like HTTP is a standard rather than a specific piece of software like Apache. What this means is that there are many implementations of servers and clients, all interactively speaking a common language from proprietary solutions to open source offerings forming a large and rich ecosystem.

The XMPP logo

XMPP provides many advantages outside of its plethora of servers and clients, which includes the following:

- **Decentralized**: Unlike big messaging silos such as MSN messenger or ICQ, XMPP is built from the ground up so that servers are able to intercommunicate, mimicking the format of the early Internet. With no single point of failure, a friend's server going down does not prevent you from communicating with other friends or colleagues.

- **Secure**: The XMPP community works hard to ensure that the standards and implementations are highly secure, by adopting things such as mandatory server-to-server encryption and secure authentication mechanisms, and by becoming involved with (and implementing where appropriate) new secure mechanisms such as **DNSSEC**. This focus on security has led to XMPP being deployed in environments requiring the highest levels of security, from actively deployed armed forces through to financial institutions.

- **Scalable**: With servers able to handle hundreds of thousands of connections at any time and due to XMPP's push architecture (versus HTTP's pull for example), hugely scaled systems not previously possible have been created.
- **Real-time**: Sending messages in real time enables new ways of developing capabilities that were previously difficult to support, such as remote collaboration on a project and talking to people all over the world without the lag or complexity of older communication methods.
- **Multi-device**: Somewhat ahead of its time, XMPP was built with multiple devices baked into the protocol. These are exposed as resources on your Jabber ID (JID), which means you can be connected to the same account from a desktop computer, a mobile phone, and a tablet at the same time and have messages routed appropriately.
- **Extensible**: XMPP is an extensible platform, meaning new functionality can be added to the protocol without interfering with existing features. This means that new ways of working and new standards come into existence (such as WebRTC), which can be integrated into XMPP with ease. These extensions are called XMPP Extension Protocols, or **XEP** for short, and a full list (including obsolete or abandoned extensions) can be seen on the XMPP website at `http://xmpp.org/ex tensions`.
- **Mature**: With hundreds of server and client implementations developed over 15 years, the standard can be said to be heavily battle-tested, and many deployments of XMPP systems demonstrate that the standards embodied by the protocol are scalable for today's Internet and the Internet of the future.

Lastly, another major advantage of using or developing on the XMPP platform is the amazing community that rallies around the protocol. Within the XSF and the community at large, there is a huge amount of experience, help, knowledge, and enthusiasm. The community has very active mailing lists, and chat rooms, as well as scores of developers writing blogs and articles and regularly speaking at events all over the world. This welcoming community means that it is easy to propose ideas, get feedback, and improve deployments or implementations with the knowledge that you will be supported by a great group of people.

# Uses of XMPP

XMPP is used to solve many real-world problems and has made its way into many large services, often without users realizing. Some large examples of deployments or XMPP-based services include:

- Jabber.org
- WhatsApp
- Google Cloud Messaging (GCM)
- Facebook chat
- Google Talk (discontinued)
- HipChat

Additionally, many services also allow users to connect via an XMPP gateway, meaning that users can connect with their preferred clients rather than with those supplied by a company, such as Slack and Skype.

XMPP is deployed in many industries where its uses go beyond simple chat applications to include diverse purposes such as the following:

- Building management
- Gaming
- System control
- Log watching
- Cyber-incident report management
- Peer-to-peer session negotiation (such as with WebRTC)
- Voice-over-IP (VoIP)
- Identity services

# XMPP and the Web

With the continuing rise of the real-time web and **WebRTC** applications, XMPP is becoming more relevant on the web than ever before. Its push architecture means that lightweight real-time applications can be built without continuously polling the server, making for more scalable web applications. Its mature standards mean that developers are quickly able to build real-world applications without having to design their own proprietary standards and benefit from the thought and problem solving that has gone into XMPP.

With all its advantages, one area that WebRTC hasn't solved (nor was it designed to solve) is the issue of session negotiation. Not only was a standard called **Jingle** available in XMPP before WebRTC arrived in the browser, but also it turns out that it's a great way of transferring session data to form peer-to-peer sessions. This means that users are now able to use WebRTC clients of their choice without having to visit and reply upon a meet me type URL or a proprietary signaling method.

# Installing Node.js and library dependencies

Node.js was released in 2009, and since its release, it has quickly become a nearly indispensable tool for server side development using JavaScript. Node.js allows developers to create fast and scalable applications (especially when asynchronous IO libraries are used) in a single language throughout an application's stack, with JavaScript running on both the back-end and front-end.

While Node.js is not required for working with XMPP, all examples in this book will utilize libraries written in Node.js, some of which can also run on the browser.

Using **Ubuntu 16.04** as a base, we're now going to install Node.js and some core dependencies for the libraries we'll be using.

First we'll install `libicu-dev` and `libexpat-dev`. These libraries allow us to perform case transformations on international characters and process XML, respectively:

```
$ sudo apt-get install libicu libexpat1-dev
```

Next, we'll work on installing Node.js itself. My preferred method of achieving this is to use `nvm` by *Tim Caswell*, which is available from this GitHub repository: `https://github.com/creationix/nvm`. Please check out the `readme` for the current installation instructions, but at the time of writing this book, the procedure is as follows:

```
$ curl https://raw.githubusercontent.com/creationix/nvm/v0.32.0
  /install.sh | bash
$ source ~/.bashrc
$ nvm install 6
$ node -v
```

This will install the latest version of the Node.js 6 release for you. The advantage of using `nvm` over the operating system packages is that it is easy to switch between different versions of Node.js with a simple command.

# Installing our XMPP server

There are a large number of XMPP servers in the wild, from proprietary to open source, with communities of varying sizes. The XSF maintains a list of servers on its website at `http://xmpp.org/xmpp-software/servers/`. However, this list does not take into account whether the projects are inactive or not; nor does it indicate the state of their implementations. Four open source servers worth having a look at which include:

- **Openfire**: A hugely popular Java-based server with a large community supporting a large number of plugins and that is actively developed (for more information can be found at: `http://www.igniterealtime.org/projects/openfire/`)
- **Tigase**: A popular Java-based server with active development and a great community, for more information can be found at `http://www.tigase.net/`
- **MongooseIM**: An Erlang-based server forked from a previous XMPP server implementation and actively developed by Erlang Solutions, which can be found at `https://github.com/esl/MongooseIM`
- **Prosody**: A fast and resource-light Lua-based server with a great core development team and an active community, which can be found at `http://prosody.im`

In this book, we're going to make use of Prosody since it is very easy to install, run, and configure. Before deploying to production, we recommend that you investigate the advantages and disadvantages of each system to see what works best for your particular requirements and environment. As XMPP is a standard, you'll be able to swap out servers without making any code changes, a great benefit of working with this setup.

# Installing the server

Installing Prosody on an Ubuntu system is very easy since it is included in the main package repositories. In order to install Prosody, run the following command at the command line:

```
$ sudo apt-get install prosody
```

Prosody can then be started and stopped using the following standard methods:

```
$ sudo service prosody start
$ sudo service prosody stop
```

If you are not using Ubuntu, then Prosody may be available via your respective package manager. The best installation instructions for Prosody can be found at `http://prosody.im/doc/install`.

Prosody also produces Docker images of their releases, which are available from the official Docker hub: `https://registry.hub.docker.com/u/prosody/prosody/`.

# Configuring the server

By default, Prosody will store its `configuration` file at `/etc/prosody/prosody.cfg.lua`. The `configuration` file itself is rather simple and is written in the **Lua** language, which is the same language in which the Prosody server is written.

Shown here is the `configuration` file we are going to use throughout this book. Following the configuration example is an explanation of each part of these settings. As always, for the most up-to-date and detailed information, please visit the Prosody website (`http://prosody.im`):

```lua
modules_enabled = {
        "roster";
        "saslauth";
        "tls";
        "dialback";
        "disco";
        "version";
        "uptime";
        "time";
        "ping",
        "register";
        "posix";
        "bosh";
};
allow_registration = true;
daemonize = true;
consider_bosh_secure = true;
cross_domain_bosh = true;
pidfile = "/var/run/prosody/prosody.pid";
c2s_require_encryption = false
authentication = "internal_plain"

log = {
        debug = "/var/log/prosody/prosody.log";
        error = "/var/log/prosody/prosody.err";
```

```
                { levels = { "error" }; to = "syslog";   };
     }

     VirtualHost "localhost"
         enabled = true
         ssl = {
             key = "/etc/prosody/certs/example.com.key";
             certificate = "/etc/prosody/certs/example.com.crt";
         }

     VirtualHost "anon.localhost"
        authentication = "anonymous"

     Component "component.localhost"
         component_secret = "mysecretcomponentpassword"
```

Now, let's discuss each of the sections of the `configuration` file:

- `modules_enabled`: describes the modules to load when Prosody is started. At its core, Prosody is quite small, but many of the XMPP features are implemented within modules. If you ask members of the Prosody team whether the server supports a new feature, the response will generally be "*There's a module for that.*" A full list of modules and configuration can be found at `http://prosody.im/doc /modules`.
- The modules we are loading here are mostly the defaults which are set by Prosody on installation:

| Module | Description |
|---|---|
| `roster` | `roster` is like an address book for XMPP. |
| `saslauth` | **Simple Authentication and Security Layer (SASL)** is a framework for authentication. It separates authentication mechanisms from application protocols, allowing any authentication mechanism supported by SASL to be used with any application protocol that uses SASL. It is within the SASL framework that we see the more secure authentication mechanisms. |
| `tls` | Transport Layer Security provides encrypted communications for XMPP data transfer. |
| `dialback` | Provides server identity verification using DNS when attempting to talk to remote servers. |
| `disco` | Short for discovery, this allows the server to advertise what features it supports to other servers and clients. |

| version | Replies to software version requests. |
|---------|----------------------------------------|
| uptime | Reports on how long the server has been active. |
| time | Reports back on the time according to the server. |
| ping | Sets up the server to reply to ping requests. |
| register | Allows clients to create new user accounts on sign-up. |
| Posix | Required for daemonizing and syslog logging. |
| Bosh | **Bidirectional-streams Over Synchronous HTTP (BOSH)** is a long polling setup that allows two way XMPP communication over HTTP. It is a predecessor of WebSockets but still very useful in situations where connectivity isn't perfect. |

- allow_registration=true;: Allow users to create an account from a client.
- daemonize = true;: Run Prosody as a daemon. If running in Docker, set this to false.
- consider_bosh_secure = true;: Generally, rather than talking to Prosody's BOSH endpoint directly, we proxy it via a web server (such as Nginx) and use that to handle SSL. Therefore it's safe to consider BOSH requests as secure.
- cross_domain_bosh = true;: This adds COR headers to BOSH responses to allow requests to come from any domain.
- pidfile = "/var/run/prosody/prosody.pid";: This is the location of the Process ID (pid) file for Prosody.
- c2s_require_encryption = false;: In production, we'd have this set to true for security, but for development, it's safe to set this to false. If set to true, then we'd be insisting on encrypted connections.
- authentication = "internal_plain";: The authentication mechanism used for clients. Here, we're saying to store the password as plain text, but in production, we'd store passwords as encrypted strings. This then also affects the usable authentication mechanisms.

- The `log` entry: Sets the log locations and the level at which we perform logging. Our setup pushes even the most detailed entries to the log files.
- Next, we define a set of virtual hosts, much like we would with a web server. Here, we have defined two virtual hosts for different reasons:
    - `VirtualHost "localhost"`: This is our main virtual host and the one on which our users will exist. A user's `JID` will appear as `test@localhost`, for example.
    - `VirtualHost "anon.localhost"`: Here we define what is known as an anonymous domain. This allows users to connect without an XMPP account. Generally, it is a best practice to prevent anonymous accounts from communicating with other servers in order to prevent spam.
- Lastly, we define a `component connection` (more about these later). We define our component to run on a subdomain. When a component attempts to connect to a server, the component sends a shared secret (i.e. a password known in configuration files for both the component and the server) as an authentication mechanism. Generally, components are run on the same server, so this method of authentication is considered appropriate.

Then we save this configuration file to `/etc/prosody/prosody.cfg.lua` and restart the server:

```
$ sudo service prosody restart
```

# Testing our setup

Next, we're going to test our Prosody setup. First, we will test whether Prosody is listening to the `client-to-server` (C2S) and `server-to-server` (S2S) ports. By default, with XMPP, the C2S port is `5222` and the S2S port is `5269`. We can perform a quick and easy test using telnet. If your server is running as expected, you will see an output similar to the following screenshot:

```
lloyd@zenbook:~$ telnet localhost 5222
Trying 127.0.0.1...
Connected to localhost.
Escape character is '^]'.
TEST C2S
<?xml version='1.0'?><stream:stream id='' xmlns:stream='http://etherx.jabber.org
/streams' version='1.0' xmlns='jabber:client'><stream:error><not-well-formed xml
ns='urn:ietf:params:xml:ns:xmpp-streams'/></stream:error></stream:stream>Connect
ion closed by foreign host.
lloyd@zenbook:~$ telnet localhost 5269
Trying 127.0.0.1...
Connected to localhost.
Escape character is '^]'.
TEST S2S
<?xml version='1.0'?><stream:stream xmlns:stream='http://etherx.jabber.org/strea
ms' xml:lang='en' xmlns:db='jabber:server:dialback' xmlns='jabber:server'><strea
m:error><not-well-formed xmlns='urn:ietf:params:xml:ns:xmpp-streams'/></stream:e
rror></stream:stream>Connection closed by foreign host.
lloyd@zenbook:~$
```

Testing Prosody connections using telnet

Next, we will also verify whether we have set up our BOSH endpoint correctly by visiting the endpoint in a browser, by visiting `http://localhost:5280/http-bind/`, port number `5280` being the default BOSH port, we should see the following screenshot:

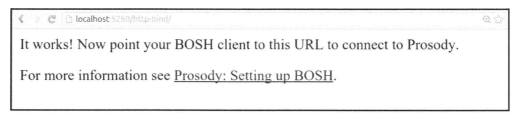

Testing Prosody's BOSH endpoint from a browser

# Creating a test account

Prosody has a great command-line utility, prosodyctl, which allows us to create and update user accounts as well as command the server. Here, we're going to use it to create our first XMPP account on the server. Type the following command in the command line:

```
$ sudo prosodyctl adduser test@localhost
```

You will then be prompted to enter a password. Let's use the Password password for now. Once this is complete, we have our XMPP account. We'll test this with a client in a moment.

 If you ever forget your user passwords, it's simply a case of running the preceding command but replacing adduser with passwd. You will then be prompted for a new password.

# Installing an XMPP client

Lastly, we'll install a standard desktop XMPP client, which will allow us to interact with our code. A list of XMPP clients is held on the XMPP website (http://xmpp.org/xmpp-softwar e/clients/). Find one suitable for your platform and follow the installation instructions.

In this book, we're going to use Empathy (https://live.gnome.org/Empathy) since it comes installed as standard in the Ubuntu desktop:

1. First, load the Empathy application and you will be presented with the main window.
2. From here, select **Accounts** from the Empathy menu in the title bar.

3. Choose to add an account and select the **Jabber** option.

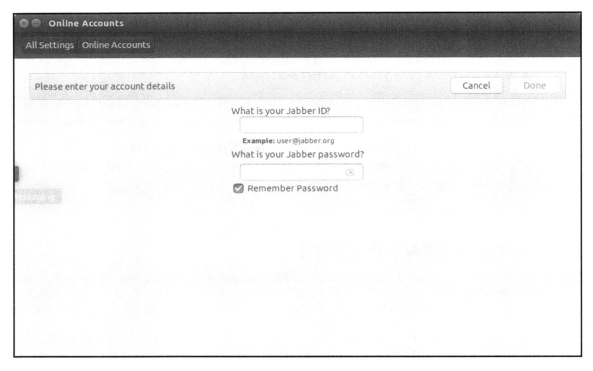

Setting up an XMPP account in Empathy on Ubuntu

4. Next, in the **Jabber ID** box, enter `test@localhost`; and for the **Password**, enter `password`.

5. Once your details are entered, pop open the **Advanced** box and uncheck **Encryption** required, since we won't need this while developing.

6. After clicking on **Done**, your client should be connected to your local XMPP server; it's not very exciting so far.

7. To doubly verify that you are connected, you can check the Prosody log file and you should see entries similar to the following:

```
$ sudo tail /var/log/prosody/prosody.log
Feb 09 20:37:43 c2s2250e30  info  Client connected
Feb 09 20:37:43 c2s2250e30  info  Authenticated as test2@localhost
```

In addition to the main log file, there is also an error log file located at `/var/log/prosody/prosody.err` (by default). Should something be happening that you aren't expecting, this is also a good location to check.

# Summary

XMPP is a widely used, secure, and federated messaging standard based on XML that has undergone a large amount of scrutiny and it is a part of the IETF.

We learned that XMPP, whilst having a very small core, can be and has been extended through additional standards called XEPs. XEPs are looked after by a group called the XMPP Standards Foundation (XSF). Because of its extensions, XMPP finds itself utilized in many scenarios, from simple multi-user chat rooms through to push notifications everyone will be familiar with from their smartphones.

We installed Node.js so that we can run the code examples that will appear later in the book. We then installed our first XMPP server (Prosody), created an account, and successfully connected to it from a traditional desktop XMPP client.

We're now ready for our adventure to begin.

In the next chapter, we'll have an overview of the core concepts from XMPP where things that you'll see often mentioned and therefore will be helpful to understand. We'll map technical concepts to more general terminology and understand why XMPP is the way it is.

Welcome to the exciting world of XMPP!

# 2
# Diving into the Core XMPP Concepts

While this book aims to get you to start building applications with XMPP quickly and effectively, it's important to understand some of the core concepts and how XMPP systems hang together. While attempting to keep things light, we'll run through these areas so that, when discussing or using XMPP, you'll understand all the terms being thrown around without having to run off to your search engine of choice.

In this chapter, we'll cover the following topics:

- Identifying yourself on the network – the JID
- The three communication blocks of XMPP
- How extensibility is achieved
- The life cycle of a connection

## Introducing the Jabber ID

In order to identify a user on the XMPP network, you need to know two things: the server on which they have an account and the account name on that server. So far, looks very much like an e-mail address, for example, `marty@mcfly.fam`.

However, XMPP being somewhat visionary for its time-realized that people would probably be using multiple devices/clients connected to the same account, and therefore added the resource that identifies a specific client connection on that account. When we include the resource, we get what is known as a full Jabber ID, or full JID. An example is `marty@mcfly.fam/highschool`.

The JID is made up of three parts:

| Local | | Domain | | Resource |
|---|---|---|---|---|
| marty | @ | mcfly.fam | / | highschool |

Like e-mail, the domain part of the JID is case insensitive, but, unlike e-mail, the local part is also case-insensitive. XMPP goes one big step beyond this, however, and uses full Unicode for addressing so that JID can be made up of any number of non-ASCII characters. To handle differences in upper or lowercase for these characters, a method called **Preparation of Internationalized Strings,** or `stringprep`, which is defined in **RFC-3454**, is used. Thankfully, this is usually implemented in lower level libraries, which makes things easier for XMPP developers.

# Message routing

By sending a message to a full JID, including the local, domain, and resource portions, you are targeting a specific connection/device on a specific account, and those messages will always go directly to the user.

If you were to send a message using the bare JID (which is a full JID without a resource), then messages to that account would be handled by the server and maybe dealt with in one of several ways. For example, the message could be forwarded to the most connected resource, or put into offline storage should there be no connections on that account.

At the very minimum, a JID must consist of a domain that would identify a server (or a component, but more on that later). Messages addressed to a domain are handled by the server itself.

# Basic building blocks of XMPP communication

This may come as a shock, but communications in XMPP come via just three (that's right three) top-level elements. These pieces of communication are called **stanzas**, and by sending sets of these with various contents, we can achieve everything we need to with XMPP. These top-level elements are:

- `<presence/>`: For sending the connection status of a client (online, offline, away, and so on)
- `<message/>`: Used to send messages or alerts
- `<iq/>`: The **Information Query**, or **IQ**, is for handling, setting and retrieval of information

In the following section, we'll talk about each of these in turn so that you can gain an overall understanding of what they are designed for and how they are used. Later in the chapter, we'll delve into XMPP communications just a little deeper, but for now let's cover these three important areas.

# `<presence/>`

Presence is all about communicating the current state or availability. If you think about IM systems, then this is the online, busy, away, or offline status of another user. For real-time communications, it is important to know whether another user is available when you send them a message so that you can (hopefully) receive a timely response.

The following is an example of a user sending their presence to their XMPP server (note that this can be achieved by not setting the `to` attribute), telling the server that they are online and ready to receive push updates. For example if Marty arrived late at school because Doc Brown set all the clocks incorrectly, he can also set a status message:

```
<presence from="marty@mcfly.fam/highschool">
  <show>available</show>
  <status>Damn alarm clocks!</status>
</presence>
```

User presence updates generally have three (all optional) children, which are as follows:

- `type`: The availability of the user. This can contain values such as **Away, Chat, Extended Away (XA),** and **Do Not Disturb (DND).**
- `status`: This is a human-readable string describing the status of the user (for example, out for lunch). There can be multiple status elements with different `xml:lang` namespaces for describing their status in several languages.
- `priority`: A value between *-127* and *+127*, which suggests to the server the connection to route messages should they be directed at the user's bare JID. Not providing a priority value automatically sets this to *0*.

Once you've sent a presence `stanza` to the server (which can be as simple as `<presence/>`), the server will start pushing real-time updates to your client.

Whenever your client updates its presence information (by sending a new presence stanza or by going offline), the server takes note. By using presence, we can also see the availability of our friends and colleagues, but first, they need to ask for permission to see our online status, and this is handled by presence subscriptions.

# Presence subscriptions

Now your presence is all very interesting, but it isn't of much use to you as you know what your current availability is. The availability of your contacts (be they friends, colleagues, family, or even some helpful bots) is much more useful. However, to see their status and for them to see yours, you must both ask and approve sharing of this information (permission is not reciprocal, and both parties must ask for and grant it). This is where presence subscriptions come in.

To ask to see another user's presence information, we must first send a request; in our case, Mr. Strickland is logged in at the Hill Valley High School office and wants to know when Marty McFly is available, so he sends a presence subscription request as follows:

```
<presence from="strickland@hillvalley.edu/office" to="marty@mcfly.fam"
type="subscribe" />
```

If Marty is online, or the next time he is online, he'll get this request pushed from the server just as before. Let's be realistic-he will probably not want to let his high school principal know his status! To avoid getting future updates about this request, he'll just tell the server no:

```
<presence from="marty@mcfly.fam/clocktower"
to="strickland@hillvalley.edu/office" type="unsubscribed" />
```

Now, if Jennifer were to send Marty a presence subscription request, I'm pretty sure he'd be willing to grant her permission, so we see these stanzas shared:

```
<presence from="jennifer@park.er/porch" to="marty@mcfly.fam"
type="subscribe" />
<presence from="marty@mcfly.fam/clocktower" to="jennifer@park.er/porch"
type="subscribed" />
```

Remember that presence subscriptions are only one-way. Marty must now ask Jennifer for permission to see her status, so he sends a request back:

```
<presence from="marty@mcfly.fam/clocktower" to="jennifer@park.er"
type="subscribe" />
```

We'll leave you to decide whether Jennifer grants Marty permission or not, but let's say she did. The next time Marty logs in with his XMPP client and sends his first presence update (which most clients will do automatically), he'll get pushed Jennifer's most recent presence status and any new updates that are sent by her clients (remembering that she could be logged in multiple times).

Should a user decide that they no longer want status updates from another user, they can unsubscribe at any time by sending an unsubscribe presence stanza:

```
<presence from="lorraine@baines.fam/underthesea" to="biff@tannen.hello"
type="unsubscribe" />
```

# Directed Presence

Some entities in XMPP aren't subscribable via Presence subscriptions, such as **publish-subscribe** (or `pubsub`) systems and multi-user chat (or MUC) rooms, so for these cases, we have what is known as **Directed Presence**.

Directed Presence is exactly the same as sending a standard presence update, but in this case, instead of setting the `to` address to that of the server (or leaving it out entirely), we set it to the JID of the receiving party. In the case of a `pubsub` system, this is likely to be a server JID; or, in the case of an MUC, we include the full JID of the room itself (more on these concepts later).

Once we've sent a Directed Presence, then once we go offline, the server will handle sending an offline notification to the JIDs to which we have sent a Directed Presence. So they stop sending us real-time updates and show us as having left the chat room (or some other appropriate behavior).

# Client capabilities

Not all XMPP clients are the same. For example, when connected from a mobile phone, the user may only wish to be involved in text chat communications, while a full desktop client may be happy to become involved in Peer-to-Peer (P2P) video and voice calls as well as file transfers. Therefore, a way to advertise the features that a client is capable of supporting is advertised using entity capabilities and is described in **XEP-0115**.

Here's a typical entity capabilities flow:

```
<presence from="doc@brown.sci/delorean">
  <c xmlns="http://jabber.org/protocol/caps"
     hash="sha-1" node="http://brown.sci/clients/outatime"
     ver="aTDVHOA1/Y8xR10p"/>
</presence>
```

In this message, the `c` element represents the capabilities that Doc's client supports. Here, the node attribute represents the client that he is using, and `ver` is a string constructed of several pieces of information about the client.

This presence is then forwarded by Doc's server to everyone who has a presence subscription. One of these people is Linda McFly, whose client doesn't recognize the `ver` string and node combination. Therefore, her client makes a query back to Doc's client to find out what capabilities it supports/provides:

```
<iq from="linda@mcfly.fam/lyonsestates"
    id="caps-query-1"
    to="doc@brown.sci/delorean"
    type="get">
  <query xmlns="http://jabber.org/protocol/disco#info"
    node="http://brown.sci/clients/outatime#aTDVHOA1/Y8xR10p"/>
</iq>
```

Here we're making a **Discovery** or DISCO request (don't worry, we'll get into DISCO requests later!), asking Doc's client to inform us what it is capable of doing. Doc's client replies as follows:

```
<iq from="doc@brown.sci/delorean"
    id="caps-query-1"
    to="linda@mcfly.fam/lyonestates"
    type="result">
  <query xmlns="http://jabber.org/protocol/disco#info"
    node="http://brown.sci/clients/outatime#aTDVHOA1/Y8xR10p"/>
    <identity category='client' name='Timeline safe XMPP Client'
    type='handheld'/>
    <feature var='http://jabber.org/protocol/caps'/>
    <feature var='http://jabber.org/protocol/disco#info'/>
    <feature var='http://jabber.org/protocol/geoloc'/>
    <feature var='urn:xmpp:time'/>
  </query>
</iq>
```

Now Linda's client knows that Doc's client supports the capability discover, the ability to discover information about the client (disco#info), Doc's geographical location, and the time of his client (very important information for time traveling!).

The next time Linda's client receives the ver and node combination, her client will understand what capabilities it supports and can thereby tailor communications with Doc appropriately. Additionally, because the ver string is generated in a standard way, should anyone else be using the same client with the same features, Linda will know what this means without querying the other clients.

# Presence overloading

Seeing the extension of presence in the preceding lines, it might seem advantageous to start adding more information to presence stanzas and extending them further. For example, Marty McFly, who listens to a lot of music, might feel it appropriate to advertise what song he is listening to from his client.

While this is perfectly achievable with XMPP, it certainly isn't a good idea. Presence stanzas form a large proportion of traffic on the XMPP network, and filling in the stanzas with additional information will greatly increase the amount of information transferred on a regular basis. Additionally, other users with presence subscriptions to Marty may not be interested in this information, and therefore it would essential be useless data being transmitted.

If this is something you are interested in doing later on, then for this we have **Personal Eventing Protocol** or **PEP** (see **XEP-0163**).

Message stanzas are the real-time update mechanisms of XMPP. At the very general level, they are most often used to pass instant messages (IM) between users; however, through the extensibility of XMPP, they can also be used to convey any structured data that a user requires alerting to.

Messages when sent do not have a built-in receipt that the message was delivered or read (although this can be achieved using XEP-0184). If a message is sent to a non-existent XMPP domain or a user that doesn't exist on a server, then an error message will be returned informing the sender of this.

Here, we see a typical message stanza sending a message from one user to another:

```
<message from="george@mcfly.fam/highschool"
to="lorraine@baines.fam/highschool" type="chat">
    <body>Lorraine. My density has brought me to you.</body>
</message>
```

Here, George is sending a private chat message to Lorraine. Should they be having a conversation, it is also possible to include a `<thread>` element containing an ID so that future messages in the conversation have context.

In this case, the type of the message is chat, but there are also several other message types:

- `groupchat`: For messages to a multi-user chat room. If a user is sending a message to a particular person in a chat room, then the type `chat` is used instead.
- `headline`: Generally used by automated systems; for example, `headline` is used by publish-subscribe systems to inform users that there is an update (often including the payload too).
- `error`: For server replies stating there was an error with message delivery.

Here is an example of a `headline` type message from a publish-subscribe system, in this case, a time update from a clock to which Doc has subscribed:

```
<message from="pubsub.clocktow.er" to="doc@brown.sci/weatherexperiment"
type="headline">
    <entry xmlns="http://www.w3.org/2005/Atom">
        <id>fc362eb42085f017ed9ccd9c4004b095</id>
        <title>Time updates</title>
```

```
        <published>1955-11-1201T22:00:00.000-8:00</published>
        <updated>1955-11-1201T22:00:00.000-8:00</updated>
        <content type="text">The time is 10:00pm</content>
        <activity:verb>post</activity:verb>
        <activity:object>
            <activity:object-type>post</activity:object-type>
        </activity:object>
    </entry>
</message>
```

While most messages will probably be of the unformatted text type in the first example, three other typical payloads include Delivery Receipts (**XEP-0184**), XHTML-formatted messages (**XEP-0071**), and chat state notifications (**XEP-0085**), which inform the receiving party about actions being performed by the other user (such as typing, pausing, and so on).

# Delivery receipts

The sending user includes an ID with each message sent, and an element requesting a delivery receipt is returned. The receiving client, upon seeing this element, returns a delivery receipt referencing this ID to the sending user:

```
<message
    from='marty@mcfly.fam/square'
    id='ack-123'
    to='doc@brown.sci/square'>
  <body>Whoa. Wait a minute, Doc. Are you trying to tell me that my mother
      has got the hots for me?</body>
  <request xmlns='urn:xmpp:receipts'/>
</message>

<message
    from='doc@brown.sci/square'
    id='msg-a4f4d9'
    to='marty@mcfly.fam/square'>
  <received xmlns='urn:xmpp:receipts' id='ack-123'/>
</message>
```

 Clients should advertise their understanding and ability to return delivery receipts via entity capabilities, as seen earlier in this chapter.

# XHTML-IM

XHTML-IM messages implement a subset of XHTML, and represent a way to share **lightweight text markup**. When sending an XHTML-IM message, note that a client should always provide a standard body element with content that best represents the information within the html element for clients that understand this extended format:

```
<message to="chuck@berry.music/phone"
from="marvin@berry.music/undertheseadance">
  <body>Chuck! Chuck, it's Marvin. Your cousin, Marvin Berry. You know that
    new sound you're looking for? Well, listen to this!</body>
  <html xmlns='http://jabber.org/protocol/xhtml-im'>
    <body xmlns='http://www.w3.org/1999/xhtml'>
      <p>Chuck! Chuck, it's Marvin. Your cousin, Marvin Berry. You know
        that <em>new sound</em> you're looking for? <strong>Well, listen to
        this!</strong></p>
    </body>
  </html>
</message>
```

# Chat state notifications

Knowing the party you are communicating with is a very useful feature in instant messaging applications and is seen throughout many different services. In XMPP, this is implemented using chat state notifications.

XMPP supports five different chat states. These are as follows:

- <active/>: The other user is actively participating in the chat or they have come back from an inactive state, for example, focusing on the chat window or returning to the computer after a break.
- <inactive/>: The other user is not actively participating in the conversation. For example, they are no longer focused on the chat window for a period of 2 minutes or more.
- <gone/>: The user is no longer participating in the chat. They may have closed the chat window or are not focused on it for a much longer period (10 minutes or more).
- <composing/>: The user is actively typing and a message may be imminent exciting times!
- <paused/>: The user was typing but has stopped, maybe to contemplate their next sentence before typing more.

In the following example, George is initially typing his response and then the message is sent with an active element stating that he is actively taking part in the conversation:

```
<message
    from='george@mcfly.fam/louscafe'
    to='biff@tannen.hello/louscafe'
    type='chat'>
  <composing xmlns='http://jabber.org/protocol/chatstates'/>
</message>
<message
    from='george@mcfly.fam/louscafe'
    to='biff@tannen.hello/louscafe'
    type='chat'>
  <body>Well of course now Biff I wouldn't want that to happen</body>
  <active xmlns='http://jabber.org/protocol/chatstates'/>
</message>
```

 As with delivery receipts, the ability to understand and send chat state notifications should be advertised by clients using entity capabilities.

The **Information Query** (IQ) stanza is where the work is done in XMPP. Rather than being used in a fire-and-forget fashion like message stanzas, IQ requests represent a request for information or a request to set some piece of information. Therefore unlike message stanzas, they always return a response, even to inform the requester of an error.

There are two types of IQ requests: The GET request, which is comparable with GET in HTTP; and the SET request, which, as you may have guessed, equates to a POST, PUT, or DELETE in HTTP. The response stanzas come in the form of RESULT or ERROR.

Unlike message or presence stanzas, IQ stanzas also have the requirement of an id attribute, which is a unique identifier that allows the mapping of a response to the original request, since XMPP is asynchronous, and so responses may be returned out of order.

A typical IQ request might be from a client to a server to see what features it supports (like our entity capabilities from before, it works on servers too!), and would look like the following:

```
<iq type='get'
    to='mcfly.fam'
    id='info-request-1' >
  <query xmlns='http://jabber.org/protocol/disco#info' />
</iq>
```

With the response being the following:

```
<iq type='result'
    from='mcfly.fam'
    to='marty@mcfly.fam/twinpinesmall'
    id='info-request=1'>
  <query xmlns='http://jabber.org/protocol/disco#info'>
    <identity category='conference' type='text' name='family-chat-rooms'/>
    <feature var='http://jabber.org/protocol/disco#info'/>
    <feature var='http://jabber.org/protocol/disco#items'/>
    <feature var='http://jabber.org/protocol/muc'/>
    <feature var='jabber:iq:time'/>
  </query>
</iq>
```

Let's say that by accident, Marty makes a request to a server that does not exist. After a short period of time, the server he is connected to will respond to him, informing him of the error. Note that the ID in the error response is exactly the same as the original stanza, and therefore Marty knows that his request for information about mcwalk.fam is related to the error that he receives in return:

```
<iq type='get'
    to='mcwalk.fam'
    id='info-request-2' >
  <query xmlns='http://jabber.org/protocol/disco#info' />
</iq>
<iq type='error'
    from='mcwalk.fam'
    to='marty@mcfly.org/pinetreesmall'
    id='info-request-2'>
  <query xmlns='http://jabber.org/protocol/disco#info'/>
  <error type='cancel'>
    <item-not-found xmlns='urn:ietf:params:xml:ns:xmpp-stanzas'/>
  </error>
</iq>
```

There's a whole set of different error response types defined for the XMPP network. These include things such as item not found, permission denied, and service unavailable. Often, errors will include an additional plain-text element describing the specific error so that the user knows exactly what has gone wrong. These errors are defined in **RFC 3920 section 3.9.2**, if you would like to read more.

While the ID attribute on a stanza should be unique and unguessable (for example, not using incrementing values), it is important that when sending IQ stanzas, clients record the address to which they are sending stanzas along with the ID to prevent what is called **stanza ID spoofing**. Without this protection, a malicious entity could take a guess at the ID of stanzas sent by your client and send, at best, bad data or, at worst, information that could reveal data that the user does not wish to share. Most XMPP clients will handle this for the user, silently protecting them from such attacks.

# Summary

In this chapter, we learned about JID, and the way users and their specific connections identify themselves on the network, as well as a little bit about message routing within XMPP.

We then went on to look at the way entities communicate, the stanza, and the three types (Presence, Message, and IQ), which between them allow for the huge range of functionality available in XMPP.

With these two core concepts understood, we can now forge ahead and start building things with XMPP with you knowing the terms that are going to be thrown around as we progress.

# 3
# Building a One-on-One Chat Bot - The "Hello World" of XMPP

Almost every programming language and framework has its own version of the "Hello World" program. XMPP frameworks are no different, and the equivalent to writing "Hello World" in XMPP is creating an echo bot, a simple XMPP client that simply returns any message it receives to the original sender.

In this chapter, we will build a simple echo bot on the server side using a `node-xmpp-client`. We will send messages to it from a standard XMPP client, and we will see the messages being echoed back. In the process, we will explore how client-to-server (C2C) streams work in XMPP.

## C2S connection life cycle

To start exchanging stanzas between the client and server, an XMPP client must first form a connection with a server and start an XML stream. XMPP servers are generally found using a **Domain Name System** (DNS) **Service record** (**SRV**). If an SRV record does not exist, the client will attempt to connect to the resolved domain directly otherwise, a hostname can be supplied by the user themselves.

Once a connection has been formed, a stream will be started using the following message:

```
<?xml version="1.0">
<stream:stream xmlns="jabber:client"
xmlns:stream="http://etherx.jabber.org/streams" version="1.0"
to="brown.sci">
```

The server will then form its own return stream with the client in response:

```
<?xml version="1.0">
<stream:stream xmlns="jabber:client"
xmlns:stream="http://etherx.jabber.org/streams" version="1.0"
from="brown.sci" id="stream:1a3f">
    <stream:features>
        <starttls xmlns="urn:ietf:params:xml:ns:xmpp-tls" />
        <compression xmns="http://jabber.or/features/compress">
            <method>zlib</method>
        </compression>
        <mechanisms xmlns="urn:ietf:params:xml:ns:xmpp-sasl">
            <mechanism>DIGEST-MD5</mechanism>
            <mechanism>PLAIN</mechanism>
        </mechanisms>
    </stream:features>
```

You will notice that the server responds with more information about the stream than it can support. In this example, it offers an encrypted connection via **Transport Layer Security (TLS)** in addition to stream compression using `zlib`. It also describes the authentication mechanisms that it will support via **Simple Authentication and Security Layer (SASL)**, which we'll cover in the next section.

Among active XMPP server administrators and server/client developers, there is an active movement to require the use of encryption in all XMPP communications as outlined in the manifesto by *Peter Saint-Andre* and documented at: `https://github.com/stpeter/manifesto/blob/master /manifesto.txt`.

Most clients will use a TLS connection if one is available. With TLS, the socket connection is upgraded without disconnecting. Within the encrypted connection, a new stream is started as in the first example.

More information on the supported stream features can be found here: `http://xmpp.org/registrar/stream-features.html`.

At the end of any XMPP session, a closing `</stream>` will be sent. This means that, you were to take the entire transcript of a connection's communications, it would comprise a well-formed XML document. The XML of the published XEP will also constitute a valid document.

# Authenticating with a server

As we saw earlier, the server stream setup response advertises a set of mechanisms by which the client can authenticate using SASL. SASL is a standard that, in theory, can support any authentication mechanism that supports the SASL standard.

Currently, you are most likely to see `PLAIN` or `DIGEST-MD5` mechanisms being advertised, but there are several others becoming more popular as awareness in security improves (for example, **SCRAM-SHA-1**). Some servers will even allow users to authenticate as an anonymous user by advertising the `ANONYMOUS` authentication mechanism.

Recall that the last portion of a fully formed JID is the resource. Once authentication has completed, the client attempts to bind its connection to that resource. A specific resource (for example, DeLorean) may be requested by the client (this, however, may be overwritten by the server), or a random resource may be supplied instead.

# Installing node-xmpp-client

To interact with an XMPP server, we will use a popular Node.js project called`node-xmpp-client`. This is a JavaScript implementation of an XMPP client that can run on both the server side or in the browser using **Browserify** (`http://browserify.org/`).

First, we will create a new folder for our project and install the library there. To do this, open a terminal window and type the following commands:

```
cd ~
mkdir xmpp-echo-bot
cd xmpp-echo-bot
npm install node-xmpp-client
```

This will install `node-xmpp-client` inside a new `node_modules` directory. At the time this book is published, `node-xmpp-client` should be at version *3.0.0* or greater.

Now we have our library installed, we start building our echo bot!

# Building our echo bot

To build our echo bot, we will need to put a few things in place. First, we will create a user account for the bot. Next, we need to let the bot connect to a server. Then we'll send and receive messages. Alright, let's build a bot!

## Creating a new user

The first thing we need to do is create an XMPP account for our bot to use. Recall from Chapter 1, *An Introduction to XMPP and Installing Our First Server* that we used `prosodyctl` to add a new account:

> `sudo prosodyctl adduser bot@localhost`

Give the account a password as `tellnoone`. Once you have created the account, you can test it using a standard XMPP client if you wish.

## Connecting to the server

Next, we'll create an `index.js` file and set up our XMPP connection:

```
const Client = require('node-xmpp-client')
const options = {
  jid: 'bot@localhost',
  password: 'tellnoone'
}
const client = new Client(options)
client.once('online', (connectionDetails) => {
  console.log('We are connected!')
  console.log(connectionDetails)
})
```

Here, we are asking to connect to the `bot@localhost` account with the password `tellnoone`. Normally, `node-xmpp-client` would perform a DNS lookup for the SRV record for the server domain, but as we're using localhost, it won't need to do that in this case. Once we create the client object, we listen for the online event that tells us that we are connected to the XMPP server and authenticated. When this event is emitted, it tells the client details about its new connection.

Should we not have DNS set up for our XMPP server (or should it not be running on localhost), then we could have specified a server parameter. Additionally, we could have requested a specific resource using a `resource` parameter on the options object, like this for example:

```
const options = {
  jid: 'bot@localhost',
  password: 'tellnoone',
  host: 'localhost',
  resource: 'echo'
}
```

Now, if we head back to our terminal and run the `index.js` script, all being well, we should see the following:

```
$ node index.js
We are connected!
{ jid:
   { local: 'bot',
     domain: 'localhost',
     resource: 'echo',
     user: 'bot' } }
```

Here, we're told that we are online and that we did in fact obtain the full JID that we requested, that is, `bot@localhost/echo`. This is a great start, but we'll have to start listening for incoming stanzas and respond with an echo if we're ever to achieve our goal!

 If you want to see exactly what is being sent back and forth between the client and server during connection and authentication, run the same script again, but with an environment variable of DEBUG equal to asterisk (*), and you'll see all the interesting details!

# Telling the server we're online

Once the client is connected, we'll need to tell the server that we're online so that it knows to route any stanzas sent to the bare JID (`bot@localhost`) through to our script. To do this, we'll need to build a stanza using the library that comes as part of `node-xmpp-client` called **Less than XML** or **ltx**

We can access `ltx` via the client object we loaded earlier. To send the presence data, we must first be online, so we'll add a function call in that event to send a presence stanza. Our code now becomes:

```
const Client = require('node-xmpp-client')
  , ltx = Client.ltx

const options = {
  jid: 'bot@localhost',
  password: 'tellnoone'
}
const client = new Client(options)
client.on('online', (connectionDetails) => {
  console.log('We are connected!')
  console.log(connectionDetails)
  sendPresence()
})

const sendPresence = () => {
  var stanza = new ltx.Element('presence')
  console.log('Sending presence: ' + stanza.toString())
  client.send(stanza)
}
```

When we run our code, we should see the following:

```
$ node index.js
We are connected!
{ jid:
   { local: 'bot',
     domain: 'localhost',
     resource: 'echo',
     user: 'bot' } }
Sending presence: <presence/>
```

Don't worry about `ltx` too much for now as we'll discuss it in more detail later.

# Listening for incoming stanzas

Next, we'll update the code to listen for incoming stanzas. This is easily done by listening for the `stanza` event on the client object we created in `index.js`. To achieve this, add the following at the end of your file:

```
client.on('stanza', (stanza) => {
  console.log('Incoming stanza: ' + stanza.toString())
})
```

Note that when we receive `stanzas` through this event, we aren't getting a raw string but a stanza parsed by the `ltx` library that gives us access to useful methods.

If we now run our script again and start sending messages to `bot@localhost` from our `test@localhost` account (connected via a standard XMPP client), we'll see the stanzas that are sent by our desktop client when attempting a conversation.

We can send messages to the bot using the **Empathy** client. In Empathy, choose **New Conversation** from the main menu. In the resulting dialog, type `bot@localhost` and hit Enter (or click on **Chat**; your call!). In the chat window, let's now say `'hello'`. In our terminal we should see the following:

```
$ node index.js
We are connected!
{ jid:
   { local: 'bot',
     domain: 'localhost',
     resource: 'echo',
     user: 'bot' }
}
Sending presence: <presence/>
Incoming stanza: <message id="41f40db8" type="chat" to="bot@localhost"
from="test@localhost/2054a4ab"
xmlns:stream="http://etherx.jabber.org/streams"><body>Hello!</body>
<active xmlns="http://jabber.org/protocol/chatstates"/><request
xmlns="urn:xmpp:receipts"/></message>
```

As we can see from the output, we were sent a chat message from Empathy with the text as expected! Great stuff! We'll also notice that Empathy is using chat state notifications as defined in **XEP-0085** (`http://xmpp.org/extensions/xep-85.html`); we'll get on to discussing these notifications later in the chapter.

# Reading the chat stanza with ltx

Next, we'll learn how to play with `ltx` in order to read the stanza using the chat message we've just received.

 `ltx` itself isn't an XMPP-specific library but a general-purpose XML parsing/building library. It can use several parsers under the same API, and will even compile and run in the browser using Browserify

First, we can determine whether the stanza was a message by using the `is()` method:

```
stanza.is('message') // === true
stanza.is('iq') // === false
```

We can also obtain the value of an element attribute by using the `attr()` method, or get a list of all the attributes by checking the `attrs` property:

```
stanza.attr('from') // ==  test@localhost/2054a4ab
stanza.attr('id') // ==  41f40db8
console.log(stanza.attrs) /*
    { id: '41f40db8',
      type: 'chat',
      to: 'bot@localhost',
      from: 'test@localhost/2054a4ab',
      'xmlns:stream': 'http://etherx.jabber.org/streams' } */
```

If we then want to see whether there was a child element called `body`, we can obtain it using:

```
const bodyElement = stanza.getChild('body')
```

Or alternatively, grab the child text from the body element using:

```
const message = stanza.getChildText('body')
const message = stanza.getChild('body').getText() /* longer alternative */
```

If the body element doesn't exist, then we'll get a null response. Therefore, it is important to verify that these elements exist before attempting to act upon them (for example, getting their text value).

There are several other methods for inspecting and retrieving data from stanzas using ltx, and these can be found in the ltx documentation available at http://node-xmpp.org/doc/ltx.html.

With this new knowledge, we can update our code to only listen for incoming chat messages and ignore other stanzas, writing out to the terminal the message content and from where it was received:

```
client.on('stanza', (stanza) => {
  if (false === stanza.is('message')) return /* Not a <message/> stanza */
  const messageContent = stanza.getChildText('body')
  if (!messageContent) return /* Not a chat message */
  const from = stanza.attr('from')
  const logEntry = 'Received message from ' ${from} ' with
    content:\n${messageContent}'
  console.log(logEntry)
})
```

If we now run our code in the terminal and send a chat message from Empathy, we should see the following output:

```
lloyd@zenbook:~/xmpp-echo-bot$ node index.js
We are connected!
{ jid:
   { local: 'bot',
     domain: 'localhost',
     resource: 'echo',
     user: 'bot' } }
Sending presence: <presence/>
Received message from test@localhost/2054a4ab with content:
Hello little chat bot!
```

# Responding to incoming messages

Now we know how to extract information from an `ltx` object. Next, we can look at building up a response stanza and echoing the message.

To start building a new stanza, we create a new message, as follows:

```
const message = new ltx.Element('message')
```

Next, we'll need to add details as to whom to send the message to and give it a type of chat. This can be achieved by using the `attr()` method and providing a second argument:

```
message.attr('type', 'chat')
message.attr('to', from) /* Since we're echoing back to the sender */
```

If we don't supply a `from` attribute, the XMPP server will be nice enough to add this data for us before passing on the stanza. By supplying a second argument to the element constructor, we can actually shortcut these method calls as follows:

```
const message = new ltx.Element(
  'message',
  { type: 'chat', to: from }
)
```

To add a child element and element text, we use the `c()` (short for child) and `t()` (short for text) methods as follows:

```
message.c('body').t(messageContent)
```

When we call `c()` on a stanza, we are returned to the child element. To move back up the XML document, we can use the `up()` method or `root()` to go back to the document root directly. When `node-xmpp-client` sends the stanza, it will always call `root()` before sending; there's no need to worry about calling this yourself first.

If we were to output the built stanza as a string, we would see this:

```
<message type="chat" to="test@localhost/2054a4ab">
<body>Hello little chat bot!</body></message>
```

We now have all the pieces required to echo messages. The last step is to send the stanza back over the client connection. This is achieved by calling the `send()` method on the client. Our final code looks like this:

```
const Client = require('node-xmpp-client')
  , ltx = Client.ltx

const options = {
  jid: 'bot@localhost/echo',
  password: 'tellnoone'
}
const client = new Client(options)
client.on('online', (connectionDetails) => {
  console.log('We are connected!')
  console.log(connectionDetails)
  sendPresence()
})

const sendPresence = () => {
  const stanza = new ltx.Element('presence')
  console.log('Sending presence: ' + stanza.toString())
  client.send(stanza)
}

client.on('stanza', (stanza) => {
  if (false === stanza.is('message')) return /* Not a <message/> stanza */
    const messageContent = stanza.getChildText('body')
  if (!messageContent) return /* Not a chat message */
    const from = stanza.attr('from')
    const logEntry = `Received message from ${from}
      with content:\n${messageContent}`
  console.log(logEntry)
    const reply = new ltx.Element(
      'message',
        { type: 'chat', to: from }
    )
  reply.c('body').t(messageContent)
    client.send(reply)
})
```

If we send a new chat message from our XMPP client, we should see our message echoed back immediately.

# Extending our echo bot

Now that we've built a simple bot, wouldn't it be nice if it were a bit more intelligent and useful? Let's extend our echo bot to do three additional things. First, we'll have it accept presence subscription requests so that users can see when the bot is online. We'll then tell it to get a result from **DuckDuckGo's Instant Answers API** (https://duckduckgo.com/api), and we'll implement chat state notifications so that it looks like the bot is thinking about the answer and responding.

# Responding to presence subscription requests

In Chapter 2, *Diving into the Core XMPP Concepts*, we introduced presence subscriptions as a way of allowing other users to see your status or availability. To make it possible for other users to see the current availability of our bot, we'll automatically approve any presence subscription requests as they are received.

Recall that a presence subscription request looks as follows:

```
<presence from="jennifer@park.er/porch" to="marty@mcfly.fam"
type="subscribe" />
```

The response is almost exactly the same (except with to/from reversed and a type of subscribed):

```
<presence from="marty@mcfly.fam/clocktower" to="jennifer@park.er/porch"
type="subscribed" />
```

Let's update our bot code to automatically respond to these requests. In addition, we'll extend our presence sending slightly to add a status (as well as a small refactor):

```
const sendPresence = () => {
  const stanza = new ltx.Element('presence')
    .c('show')
    .t('available')
  console.log('Sending presence: ' + stanza.toString())
  client.send(stanza)
}
const handleMessage = (stanza) => {
  const messageContent = stanza.getChildText('body')
  if (!messageContent) return /* Not a chat message */
  const from = stanza.attr('from')
  const reply = new ltx.Element(
    'message',
    { type: 'chat', to: from }
```

```
    )
    reply.c('body').t(messageContent)
    client.send(reply)
}
const handlePresence = (stanza) => {
    if (false === stanza.attr('subscribe')) {
        return /* We don't handle anything other than a subscribe */
    }
    const reply = new ltx.Element(
        'presence',
        { type: 'subscribed', to: stanza.attr('from') }
    )
    client.send(reply)
}
client.on('stanza', (stanza) => {
    if (true === stanza.is('message')) {
        return handleMessage(stanza)
    } else if (true === stanza.is('presence')) {
        return handlePresence(stanza)
    }
})
```

This is great progress! Now other users (once requested) will be able to see if the bot is online and responding to requests!

# Returning results from DuckDuckGo Instant Answers API

Our next step is to make the bot do something more useful than to just echo back the original request. We'll have the bot use the user's message as a query for the DuckDuckGo Instant Answers API and simply return the first result URL and description.

As this is Node.js, there's already a useful library (https://github.com/jawerty/node-ddg) that wraps up all the required requests and returns the information we are after. To install this library, we run this from our terminal within the project folder:

```
$ npm install ddg
```

At the top of our bot script, we then load the library by including the following line:

```
const ddg = require('ddg')
```

Next, we update our `handleMessage()` function to make a library call:

```
const handleMessage = (stanza) => {
  const query = stanza.getChildText('body')
  if (!query) return /* Not a chat message */
  const from = stanza.attr('from')
  ddg.query(query, (error, data) => {
    const result = null
    if (error) {
      result = 'Unfortunately we could not answer your request'
    } else {
      if (!data.RelatedTopics[0]) {
        result = 'Sorry, there were no results!'
      } else {
        const item = data.RelatedTopics[0]
        result = item.FirstURL + '\n' + item.Text
      }
    }
    const reply = new ltx.Element(
      'message',
      { type: 'chat', to: from }
    )
    reply.c('body').t(result)
    client.send(reply)
  })
}
```

Now, if we fire up our bot script again, we'll see some interesting results when we send it some messages:

# Sending chat state notifications

Now our bot is actually doing some useful work for us! The last step is to give the user some indication that it is doing something. In order to do this, we'll use**Chat State Notifications** (**XEP-0085**: `http://xmpp.org/extensions/xep-85.html`)

These notifications are designed to indicate to your chat partner when you are typing, paused, inactive, and so on so that they know whether to expect a reply in the near future. This is a common pattern seen in many chat applications. Here's how it is implemented in XMPP.

Chat state notifications have five possible values, which are as follows:

- `<active/>`: The user is actively participating in the conversation.
- `<inactive/>`: The user is no longer actively participating in the conversation. For example, they've unfocussed the chat window, or have been away from their computer for a couple of minutes or more.
- `<gone/>`: The user is no longer participating in the conversation at all. For example, they've been away from their computer for a period of 10 minutes or more.
- `<composing/>`: The user is composing a reply.
- `<paused/>`: The user was composing a reply but has temporarily paused.

Chat state notifications can be sent by themselves as in the following:

```
<message to="marty@mcfly.fam/delorean" to="doc@brown.sci/delorean"
type="chat">
  <composing xmlns='http://jabber.org/protocol/chatstates'/>
</message>
```

They can also be sent as part of the chat message itself:

```
<message to="marty@mcfly.fam/deloean" to="doc@brown.sci/clocktowner"
type="chat">
  <body>Come on Doc!</body>
  <inactive xmlns='http://jabber.org/protocol/chatstates'/>
</message>
```

The ability to support chat state notifications should be advertised by a client using the `http://jabber.org/protocol/chatstates` namespace upon a `disco#info` request. This is purely a client feature, and therefore no support is required from the server. For a list of Jabber namespaces, see `http://xmpp.org/registrar/namespaces.html`.

For our bot, it would be great if we could let the request or know that the bot is active in the conversation, then composing a response while the server request is sent, and then inactive when the result is sent.

In the `active` and `composing` states, we'll send just the state notification to the requester, and then, once we've sent our response, we'll include the `inactive` along with the result:

```
const NS_CHAT_STATE = 'http://jabber.org/protocol/chatstates'
const sendChatState = (to, state) => {
  const stanza = new ltx.Element('message', { type: 'chat', to })
  stanza.c(state, { xmlns: NS_CHAT_STATE })
  console.log('Sending chat state: ' + stanza.toString())
  client.send(stanza)
}
const handleMessage = (stanza) => {
  const query = stanza.getChildText('body')
  if (!query) return /* Not a chat message */
  const from = stanza.attr('from')
  sendChatState(from, 'active')
  sendChatState(from, 'composing')
  ddg.query(query, (error, data) => {
    const result = null
    if (error) {
      result = 'Unfortunately we could not answer your request'
    } else {
      if (!data.RelatedTopics[0]) {
        result = 'Sorry, there were no results!'
      } else {
        const item = data.RelatedTopics[0]
        result = item.FirstURL + '\n' + item.Text
      }
    }
    const reply = new ltx.Element(
      'message',
      { type: 'chat', to: from }
    )
    reply.c('body').t(result)
      .up()
      .c('inactive', { xmlns: NS_CHAT_STATE })
    console.log('Sending response: ' + reply)
    client.send(reply)
  })
}
```

Notice that when building the stanza that includes the query result, we use the `up()` method, since a `c()` call always returns the child element.

Now, by running our bot and sending a request, we should see the following in the terminal:

```
$ node index-ddg.js
We are connected!
{ jid:
   { local: 'bot',
     domain: 'localhost',
     resource: 'echo',
     user: 'bot' } }
Sending presence: <show>available</show>
Sending chat state: <message type="chat" to="test@localhost/2054a4ab">
<active xmlns="http://jabber.org/protocol/chatstates"/></message>
Sending chat state: <message type="chat" to="test@localhost/2054a4ab">
<composing xmlns="http://jabber.org/protocol/chatstates"/></message>
Sending response: <message type="chat" to="test@localhost/2054a4ab">
<body>https://duckduckgo.com/c/Films_directed_by_Robert_Zemeckis
 Films directed by Robert Zemeckis</body>
<inactive xmlns="http://jabber.org/protocol/chatstates"/></message>
```

# Signing off

Ideally, just before closing our client connection, we should send a presence to the server to tell it that we are going offline, as follows:

```
<presence type='unavailable'/>
```

However, XMPP servers will generally send this to all your contacts when it detects that your client connection is closed on your behalf (including those contacts you've sent a directed presence to).

# Summary

Great work! In this chapter, we've learned a huge amount! We wrote code to connect to an XMPP server, handle incoming messages and presence subscriptions, inspect and build stanzas, and send chat state notifications.

Ultimately, we've built a useful bot that heads off and fetches information about subjects from DuckDuckGo's API. It's not hard to see how we can extend this concept to also do lots of other useful tasks, from being a highly secure calculator (because everyone needs one of those!) to being able to run commands remotely on a server based on incoming messages. The world, as they say, is your oyster!

In the next chapter, we are going to learn about a library called XMPP For The Web (XMPP-FTW), which will help us build browser-based applications including browser-based chat applications, which we will explore in subsequent chapters.

# 4
# Talking XMPP in the Browser Using XMPP-FTW

The Internet is everywhere and no longer is it safe to assume that an application is something you download and install. More and more applications come in the form of web applications or web apps, and as this book has *Practical* in the title it would be outrageous not to move our server tools to the browser and build cool stuff from there.

In this chapter, we'll look at the traditional ways of interacting with XMPP in the browser, discover why it is difficult, and get to know and install **XMPP For The Web** (XMPP-FTW). Then we'll look at starting a conversation with the echo bot we created in **XMPP-FTW**). Then we'll look at starting a conversation with the echo bot we created in Chapter 3, *Building a One-on-One Chat Bot – The "Hello World" of XMPP*.

## Interacting with XMPP in the browser

When XMPP was first developed, the standard way to use software was to install an application on your home computer and connect to the Internet over a 56k modem. Browsers were devices for visiting simple text and image documents linked together by hyperlinks. Some people still refer to it as an *information superhighway*.

For this reason, while XMPP has been used in web applications in various ways, it has somewhat been overlooked. Web developers in general have had bad experiences with XML or see it as unnecessarily verbose (especially next to JSON).

With the rise of the real time web, the proliferation of a new wave of chat, the **Internet of Things (IoT)**, and WebRTC applications (all discussed in Chapter 10, *Real-world deployment and XMPP Extensions*), we see XMPP becoming increasingly more relevant and popular. As a proven system, it has solved the problems these applications face in terms of scalability and security it has well as also provided a standards-based method to avoid vendor lock-in.

Let's take a look at the two different methods of speaking to an XMPP server: One based on our old friend HTTP and another using a more recent WebSocket specification.

# BOSH

**Bidirectional-Streams Over Synchronous HTTP**, or **BOSH** (for more information on the specification, visit http://xmpp.org/extensions/xep-124.html), is the XMPP name for a long polling style of interacting in real time with the browser. It uses or some would say abuses-standard HTTP to expose something akin to two-way real time communication between a client and a server.

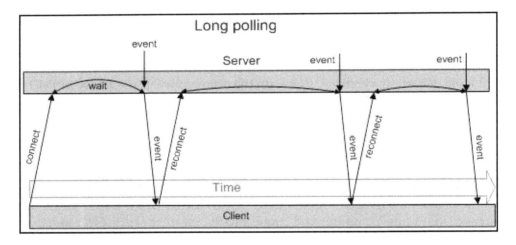

BOSH works by opening a connection to the server and sending a stanza wrapped in a <body/> element (if required). The server will then hold open the connection until such time as it has something to send to the client, at which time it will send the stanza (again wrapped) and close the connection. The client will then re-establish a new connection immediately. If, until some predetermined timeout elapses (generally around 60 seconds), there is no stanza to send to the client, then the server will close the connection, again with the client re-establishing a connection immediately.

Each connection has a related session ID (`sid`) and request ID (`rid`), which allow the BOSH server to relate an HTTP session with an XMPP session on the backend.

While using HTTP may seem very old fashioned compared to something as modern as a WebSocket (which we'll cover next), it does have the advantage of being very tolerant of unreliable networks as new connections are made and destroyed on a regular basis.

# The WebSocket protocol

The WebSocket protocol started appearing in browsers in the late 2000 and became an IETF standard in 2011. Once a handshake is negotiated over HTTP, it creates an interactive TCP connection between a server and a browser, allowing for interactive communications with very little overhead. At this point, it no longer bears any resemblance to standard HTTP.

Having a full, two-way open connection between the server and the browser allows much faster and closer to real time communications for web applications. The XMPP WebSocket API was standardized by the IETF in 2014 (for more information, see `https://datatracker.ietf.org/doc/rfc7395/`) and is now implemented by all of the most popular XMPP servers.

While WebSockets do have the advantages of lower latency and higher throughput, they also have a disadvantage that if the connection is severed, the connection between the server and the browser IT needs to be reconnected and the XMPP client connection must be renegotiated. Therefore, it is not reliable for situations where connections unreliable. This can be overcome with some work by implementing stream management and session resumption techniques (for more information on **session management**, refer to `http://xmpp.org/extensions/xep-198.html`), which were originally developed for the BOSH protocol. However, this isn't built in as it is with BOSH.

# Introducing XMPP-FTW

Around the autumn of 2012, as the real-time web was really starting to become an important area, members of the XMPP developer community recognized that developer teams were generating a lot of their own proprietary message setups but, more importantly, were making the same mistakes that had already been solved in XMPP over a decade earlier. The problem is that web developers simply saw XMPP and immediately sought simpler solutions.

Most of the issues arose from having to work with XML. It is not a format that is familiar to most web-developers; developers simply had bad experiences with it (remember SOAP?) or WebSockets were not available and BOSH just seemed slow and cumbersome.

The solution was to deliver an alternative interface to XMPP. Naturally, for the Web, this was JSON over a WebSocket. On the surface, this appears to be an easy goal since many people think, incorrectly, that you can cleanly translate back and forth between XML and JSON. Sadly, all existing attempts at this result in the one thing worse than XML ugly JSON!

Some work was started at an XSF meeting in Brussels in February 2013 and this piece of exploratory work actually spawned two projects. The first is XMPP-FTW and the second is **Stanza.io** (http://stanza.io) by *Lance Stout*.

The two projects differ in that XMPP-FTW is event-based and requires a server-side component to manage the WebSocket connection, whereas stanza.io is a purely client side API solution with the then-draft WebSocket implementation added to the Prosody XMPP server.

XMPP-FTW does not attempt to cover all of XMPP but a subset (although, it can be extended and the amount of XEPs covered is increasing). It uses patterns that are seen through the various standards, and attempts to keep things as simple as possible while still giving access to as much of the underlying functionality as possible. That said, it does not attempt to handhold the developer through XMPP.

The library itself is actually made up of over 23 small modules that implement different parts of the various standards and can be included or left out to support only the functionality the developer would like to expose to the browser.

Additionally, it doesn't prescribe a transport mechanism. This is something the developer provides to the library so that it could quite happily work with WebSockets, HTTP, telnet, or even crazier transport mechanisms such as e-mail! In reality, we use a WebSocket library such as `socket.io` (`http://socket.io`), SockJS (`https://github.com/sockjs`), or any other Node.js WebSocket implementation. The demo project (`https://docs.xmpp-ftw.org`) uses `socket.io` behind the WebSocket abstraction layer **Primus** (`http://primus.io`).

The reason for the separation of the transport and the library is so that developers can use their preferred transport, and also WebSocket libraries take care of things like disconnections and reconnections much better than a custom library. Primus further allows developers to choose a WebSocket library that suits their infrastructure and traffic needs best without changing any code.

Once a WebSocket connection is formed, the server will hold a TCP connection open to the XMPP server on the user's behalf (it uses `node-xmpp-client` for this), binding the two together. When the library receives a stanza from the server, it will interpret the data, convert it to JSON, and emit an appropriate event (all events begin xmpp to prevent clashes). If an event is received from the WebSocket connection, the library will build the appropriate stanza and send it to the XMPP server, registering a callback function as appropriate.

We'll see how this works in practice as we work through the example code to follow.

# Installing XMPP-FTW

The easiest way to get started with XMPP-FTW is to check out the skeleton project from GitHub. We'll then go through each part of the server code to explain what is happening:

```
cd ~
git clone git@github.com:xmpp-ftw/skeleton-project.git xmpp-ftw
cd xmpp-ftw
npm i
```

The skeleton project you've installed is a simple application that simply anonymously logs in to the **Buddycloud** (`http://buddycloud.com`) demo social network application, pulls the latest posts from their developer channel, and puts them into the web page.

If you now open up the `index.js` file, you'll see what is happening:

```
const express    = require('express')
  , Emitter      = require('primus-emitter')
  , Primus       = require('primus')
  , engine       = require('ejs-locals')
  , xmpp         = require('xmpp-ftw')
  , Buddycloud = require('xmpp-ftw-buddycloud')
```

Here we're just loading a set of modules. Express is a simple web server for Node.JS, `primus` and `primus-emitter` are libraries related to the WebSocket abstraction layer, `ejs-locals` is a simple templating system used with Express, and `xmpp-ftw` and `xmpp-ftw-buddycloud` are the two modules we are going to use to interact with XMPP.

The main `XMPP-FTW` library contains implementations for simple one-to-one chat, presence, and roster, as well as a set of useful smaller utilities (such as code to work with data forms can be found at `http://xmpp.org/extensions/xep-4.html`). Additionally, it includes the main parent code as well as a base class from which all `XMPP-FTW` libraries should extend.

Continuing our look through `index.js`:

```
const app = express()
app.get('/', function(req, res) {
    res.render('index')
})
const server = app.listen(3000, function() {
    console.log('Listening on port %d', server.address().port)
})
```

Here we're setting up the web server and telling it to render the `index.ejs` file from our `views` directory:

```
app.configure(function() {
    app.use(express.static(__dirname + '/public'))
    app.set('views', __dirname + '/views')
    app.set('view engine', 'ejs')
    app.use(express.bodyParser())
    app.use(express.methodOverride())
    app.use(express.logger)
    app.use(express.errorHandler({
        dumpExceptions: true,
        showStack: true
    }))
    app.engine('ejs', engine)
})
```

The preceding code is simply configuration for the server. The important part is the line that includes `express.static`. This line tells the server that if a file exists in a `public` directory, then it should serve it directly:

```
const options = {
    transformer: 'socket.io',
    parser: 'JSON',
    transports: [
        'websocket',
        'htmlfile',
        'xhr-polling',
        'jsonp-polling'
    ]
}
const primus = new Primus(server, options)
primus.use('emitter', Emitter)
primus.save(__dirname + '/public/scripts/primus.js')
```

Now we're starting to get to the interesting part of the code, although there isn't much code at all, which is one of the best parts of setting this up! Here, we're creating an instance of `primus` (the WebSocket abstraction layer). First, we set up the options to use the `socket.io` WebSocket library, with JSON payloads, and we'd like to use the four different specified transport mechanisms, from super-fast, super-modern WebSockets right back to good old polling mechanisms (great for devices with poor connectivity or behind firewalls!).

Lastly, we connect it to the web server, tell `primus` to use the emitter plugin we loaded earlier (`primus-emitter`), and tell it to save its client code to the public directory, which is where the files to be served are located:

```
primus.on('connection', function(socket) {
    console.log('Websocket connection made')
    const xmppFtw = new xmpp.Xmpp(socket)
    xmppFtw.addListener(new Buddycloud())
    socket.xmppFtw = xmppFtw
})

primus.on('disconnection', function(socket) {
    console.log('Client disconnected, logging them out')
    socket.xmppFtw.logout()
})
```

The final lines of the code actually see us loading XMPP-FTW. Here, we're detecting a new WebSocket connection, loading an instance of XMPP-FTW, and injecting the BuddyCloud extension. Upon disconnection, we also call the logout method of the XMPP-FTW instance so that the appropriate messages are sent to the server.

That's in a whole web-accessible XMPP-FTW server in *~50* lines of code.

# Playing with XMPP-FTW using the demo application

One of the best ways to start exploring XMPP-FTW is, in fact, not to run any code at all but to interact with XMPP manually via the projects demo console, which can be found at `http://docs.xmpp-ftw.org/demo`:

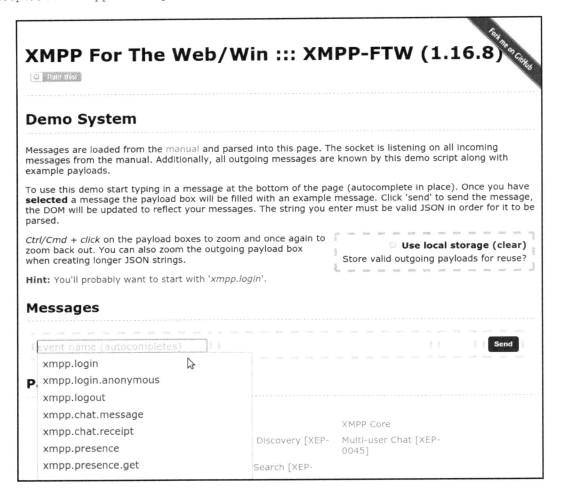

The demo client, upon loading, creates a secure WebSocket connection back to a full instance of XMPP-FTW (including all the current extensions).

After loading, the client will retrieve data from each of the manual pages to pull in the XMPP events you can see listed in the dropdown on the left-hand side. Additionally, it will also register all incoming events, so any received stanzas will appear in the demo.

By loading the event data from the manual itself, we can be assured that the events being generated are exhaustive and are using the latest message formats.

The manual pages themselves can be found at `https://docs.xmpp-ftw.org/manual` and are also linked from the footer.

If you'd like to play with the demo client itself, it can be downloaded from `https://github.com/xmpp-ftw/xmpp-ftw-demo` or installed from NPM as follows:

```
npm i xmpp-ftw-demo
```

The website is running the latest code available from the NPM repository at all times.

We'll now go through a quick example in which we log in to an XMPP server, discover what features the server supports, and make a ping request to the server.

No XMPP account? If you currently do not have an XMPP account on a public server already, then why not?! To remedy this obvious mistake, we suggest heading to the IM observatory's public server listing page (`https://xmpp.net/directory.php`) and signing up with an account on one of the A-graded servers. Each server's registration procedure will differ, so please visit their website for details. Welcome to the wider world of XMPP!

First, we'll need to log in to our XMPP account. To do this start, typing the name of the event for login in the first gray-bordered area under the **Messages** heading. The event we are looking for is `xmpp.login`. By clicking on the event name, you'll notice that the demo application has dropped an example payload into the box to the right, ready for us to substitute our login details in.

Too small? You can try `Ctrl plus click` on the payload (and response payload) text boxes to see a larger version. Press `Ctrl plus click` again to shrink the magnified view.

## Messages

xmpp.login

```
{
"jid": "test@evilprofessor.co.uk",
"password": "password",
/* "resource": "xmpp-ftw", */
/* "host": "127.0.0.1" */
}
```

No    **Send**

Now you'll need to enter your valid login details (you can almost certainly remove the **resource** and **host** fields). Once complete, hit the **Send** button, and within a very short time you should see a message saying you are successfully logged in (note that you'll need to write valid JSON for the client to parse your input).

xmpp.connection

```
{
"status": "online",
"jid": {
"local": "lloyd",
"domain": "buddycloud.org",
"resource": "b3f008e8-2600-4877-8dbe-96f105f01f2a",
"user": "lloyd"
}
}
```

Repeat, repeat, repeat! If you start playing with demo client on a regular basis, you may find it very boring to keep typing in common stanza data. The developers of the demo anticipated your pain and added the `Use local storage` checkbox, which saves outgoing stanzas to your browser. With the box checked, the next time you click on an event to send, it will populate the data from your storage rather than the example payload. Win, right?

Now that we're connected, we'll run a quick feature discovery request to our server and see what features it has available. For this, we'll need to start typing `xmpp.discover.info`, and select the appropriate event. You can also see `http://xmpp.org/extensions/xep-4.h tml` and `https://xmpp-ftw.jit.su/manual/service-discovery` for more details about discovery requests. Recall that we learned about discovery requests in `Chapter 2`, *Diving into the Core XMPP Concepts*.

Let's first do something that's a little strange and purposefully a little wrong. In the payload box, simply enter an empty JSON object (`{ }`) and hit **Send**. You should see the following as the output:

```
xmpp.discover.info          {}                      {
                                                      "type": "modify",
                                                      "condition": "client-error",
                                                      "description": "Missing 'of'
                                                    key",
                                                      "request": {}
                                                    }
```

What this is showing us is that we can easily link an incoming response event to its original outgoing event (we'll do this in code later) and that the demo client will show this in the appropriate location for us.

Next, let's fix our outgoing payload and get a more appropriate response. Now, as we're on a public XMPP network, we don't just have to speak to the server we have connected to. Therefore, we'll run our feature discovery request against one of the biggest and most popular XMPP services there is, namely `Jabber.org`. For this, our JSON payload should be entered as follows with the `xmpp.discover.info` event:

```
{ "of": "jabber.org" }
```

Hitting **Send** should result in the following as output (note that I've used `Ctrl plus click` on the response to maximize the data):

Awesome stuff, right? Now we're not only communicating with an XMPP server using JSON from a browser, but also using the federated nature of XMPP to talk to a remote server and find out what services it provides. Super awesome!

```json
[
  {
    "kind": "identity",
    "type": "im",
    "name": "Isode M-Link 16.3v3",
    "category": "server"
  },
  {
    "kind": "identity",
    "type": "pep",
    "category": "pubsub"
  },
  {
    "kind": "identity",
    "type": "user",
    "category": "directory"
  },
  {
    "kind": "feature",
    "var": "jabber:iq:search"
  },
  {
    "kind": "feature",
    "var": "jabber:iq:version"
  },
  {
    "kind": "feature",
    "var": "urn:xmpp:ping"
  },
  {
    "kind": "feature",
    "var": "http://jabber.org/protocol/disco#info"
  },
  {
    "kind": "feature",
    "var": "http://jabber.org/protocol/disco#items"
  },
  {
    "kind": "feature",
    "var": "http://jabber.org/protocol/commands"
  },
  {
    "kind": "feature",
    "var": "vcard-temp"
  }
]
```

If you now look through the list of features, you'll notice that one of them has a feature of `urn:xmpp:ping`, which means we can ping the server. So let's do that!

To ping the XMPP server, we need the simple event called `xmpp.ping` (for more details on XMPP ping, see `http://docs.xmpp-ftw.org/manual/ping`) and hit the **Send** button. We should get an almost instant reply of **true**:

```
xmpp.ping          {                     true
                     "to": "jabber.org"
                   }
```

If you are really interested in the timings of the communications, then, if you pop open the developer tools in your favorite browser, you'll see log messages about communication times.

In my case, I'm sitting at a desk in the southwest of the UK, talking to the demo server on the East Coast of the USA (via a WebSocket), which is talking to a server in the south of Germany (via a C2S socket), which itself is then talking to a server in the mid-US (via an S2S socket), and then bouncing all the way back. So that's six trips across the Atlantic in a very short span of time. Obviously, when deployed, you'd install your own instance and put everything as close together as possible, but isn't technology just amazing?

# Talking to our bot from the browser

So now you've learned about XMPP connections and XMPP-FTW, and you have played with a JSON-based XMPP interface in a browser. Now let's build a very simple chat client to talk to the bot we wrote in `Chapter 3`, *Building a One on One Chat Bot – The "Hello World" of XMPP*.

# Building a WebSocket-enabled web server in Node.js

First, let's create a new folder and initialize a new NPM project:

```
mkdir browser-chat && cd browser-chat
npm init
```

Answer the questions however you wish (you can just happily accept all the defaults if you want). Once completed, you'll have a saved `package.json` file that describes the project. As we install modules, we'll write their details into the file so that the installations can be repeated by others later.

Rather than use express, we're going to use the base HTTP module from Node.js, as we're only looking to deliver a couple of static assets from the server itself. Create a file called `index.js` using an editor of your choice and add the following:

```
const http = require('http')
const server = http.createServer((req, res) => {
  res.write('XMPP rocks my cotton socks!')
  res.end()
})
server.listen(3000)
```

Please feel free to contact the author for the usual `vim` versus `emacs` editor discussion, but be aware that `vim` is always the correct answer!

In the preceding code, we're creating an HTTP server and telling it to listen to port 3000. When a request (`req`) is received, we simply write our string to the response (`res`) object and close the connection.

If we now save and exit the file, then by running node `index.js` and opening our browser to `http://localhost:3000`, we should see a browser window that looks like this:

Next, we'll want to extend the code to return some static files (namely an `index.html` and some JavaScript files) to the user. We'll write it such that if a file exists on the filesystem, we'll return an HTTP status code of *200*, set a MIME-type of text/html (unless the file is in a scripts directory, in which case we'll return application/Javascript), and return the file contents. However, if the file is not found on the filesystem, then we'll just return a simple *404* response. OK, let's dive in…

```
cosnt http = require('http')
  , fs = require('fs')
  , path = require('path')
  , url = require('url')
const server = http.createServer((req, res) => {
  const uri = url.parse(req.url).pathname
  if (uri === '/') uri = '/index.html'
  const filename = path.join(process.cwd(), 'public', uri)
  fs.exists(filename, function(exists) {
    if (!exists) {
      res.writeHead(404)
      res.end()
```

```
      return
    }
    const mimeType = (-1 === req.url.indexOf('/scripts')) ?
      'text/html' : 'application/javascript'
    res.writeHead(200, mimeType)
    fs.createReadStream(filename).pipe(res)
  })
})
server.listen(3000)
```

In this example, we load a set of useful modules, with `fs` handling filesystem interactions, `path` helping us to build file system paths, and `url` helping us to parse incoming URLs. Next, we use the path module to obtain the requested URL path; if the value is simply a slash, then we'll assume the user is requesting an `index.html` file for convenience. After this, we use the `fs` module to see whether the file exists on the system after building up a filesystem path from the processes working directory, a public subfolder, and the original requested file. Given that Node.js tries not to block on Input/Output (IO), this is an asynchronous callback.

If this file does not exist, then we write an HTTP status code of *404* (not found) to the headers and end the request. But if the file is found, we check for the existence of script in the request URL and set our MIME-type response accordingly as well as a *200* (OK) response code. Lastly, we load the file from the filesystem and pipe it into our response.

Got that? Groovy! Then let's continue. If we create ourselves a public folder, generate an `index.html` file, and fire the server back up, we should see our HTML being sent to the browser:

```
mkdir -p public/scripts
echo "<h1>XMPP rocks everyone's socks</h1>" > public/index.html
node index.js
```

Refreshing our browser should return the expected message. Also note that if you navigate to an unknown URL, for example, `http://localhost:3000/does-not-exist`, you'll get a `not found` error in your browser.

Let's get cracking with our WebSocket connection! To do that, we'll first install a library called `primus` (`http://primus.io`). Primus is a WebSocket abstraction layer for the, well, common Node.js WebSocket abstraction layers, but it has a huge benefit of unifying their APIs and fixing some bugs in the underlying code. We're also going to make use of the `ws` WebSocket library (which is probably the simplest library you'll find). To install these and save them to our `package.json` file, we run the following:

```
npm install --save primus@2 ws
```

If you quickly pop open your `package.json` file, you'll note that both of these dependencies have been written inside, making it easy to install the same modules later using `npm` install in the same directory.

Now we'll add primus to our script and handle a new WebSocket connection and disconnection. To make things simpler, we'll simply add our new code at the end of `index.js`:

```
const Primus = require('primus')
const options = { transformer: 'websockets' }
const primus = new Primus(server, options)
primus.on('connection', (socket) => {
  console.log('New websocket connection')
})
primus.on('disconnection', (socket) => {
    console.log('Websocket disconnected')
})
primus.save(path.join(process.cwd(), 'public', 'scripts', 'primus.js'))
```

Here, we're generating a new Primus object, linking it to our server, and then reporting on new connections and disconnections. Primus will also generate the appropriate client side code for us, which we'll save to the `public/scripts` directory.

# Talking WebSockets from a browser

Now that we have our server all set up to listen for WebSocket connections, we can start building our browser code. For this, we'll pull in a Primus client code and update our `index.html` to create the WebSocket connection. Our HTML file now becomes:

```
<!DOCTYPE html>
<html>
<head>
  <title>XMPP Client Example</title>
  <script type="text/javascript" src="/scripts/primus.js"></script>
  <script type="text/javascript">
  const socket = new Primus()
  socket.on('open', function() {
    console.log('Websocket connection achieved!')
  })
  </script>
  <script type="text/javascript" src="/scripts/xmpp.js"></script>
</head>
<body>
  <h1>Instant Answers Example Client</h1>
```

```
   <p>Send me a search question and I'll reply with an answer</p>
</body>
</html>
```

Firing up your web server once again and peeking at both its output and the browser developer console, you should now see messages about WebSocket connections being created. Hit refresh in the browser and you'll also see a note about the previous connection being closed before another is reopened. Exciting stuff!

# Installing XMPP-FTW and getting messaging!

The last step for our server code is to install XMPP-FTW and wire it up on the server side. But before that, we need a `primus` plugin called`primus-emitter` (https://github.com/c ayasso/primus-emitter), which allows us to use an event emitter with the WebSocket:

```
npm i --save primus-emitter@3
```

Then we append `index.js` with the following before `primus.save()` to tell primus make use of the plugin:

```
primus.use('emitter', require('primus-emitter'))
```

Finally, we can install `XMPP-FTW` on the server side and start concentrating on the client:

```
npm i --save xmpp-ftw
```

Now, within our WebSocket connection blocks, we'll need to create and destroy our `XMPP-FTW` sessions, as follows:

```
const Xmpp = require('xmpp-ftw')
primus.on('connection', (socket) => {
  console.log('New websocket connection')
  const xmpp = new Xmpp.Xmpp(socket)
  socket.xmpp = xmpp
})
primus.on('disconnection', (socket) => {
  console.log('Websocket disconnected, logging user out')
  socket.xmpp.logout()
})
```

`XMPP-FTW` by default includes extensions to handle both one-to-one chat and presence, so there's no additional code to put in at this point. Now, to the client!

# Chatting with our XMPP bot

To chat with our bot, we'll need three sets of areas on our web page. To make the development process easier, we'll import jQuery into our web page. To do this, we'll add a script tag to our `<head>` section and pull in jQuery (`http://jquery.com/`) from the **Google CDN**:

```
<script
src="https://ajax.googleapis.com/ajax/libs/jquery/2.1.4/jquery.min.js">
</script>
```

Then for our page elements, we'll first add a simple login form:

```
<div class="login">
  <label for="jid">JID</label><input type="text" name="jid"
   placeholder="jid" />
  <label for="password">Password</label><input type="password"
   name="password" />
  <p class="connection-status">Offline</p>
  <button type="button" name="login">Login</button>
</div>
```

Then we'll add an area to send our messages from:

```
<div class="send">
  <label for="outgoing-message">Message</label>
  <textarea name="outgoing-message"></textarea>
  <button type="button" name="send-message">Send Message</button>
</div>
```

Lastly, we'll add an area to hold incoming messages:

```
<div class="received"></div>
```

# Login

The first task we'll need to complete is to get logged in to our server. Let's create a script file in our project at `public/scripts/xmpp.js`, where we can start handling the client side features. To handle login, we'll listen for a client on the login button:

```
socket.on('xmpp.connection', connected)
var connected = function(details) {
  $('p.connection-status').html('Online')
}
socket.on('xmpp.error', errorReceived)
var errorReceived = function(error) {
  if ('auth' === error.type) {
    return alert('Authentication failed')
  }
}
$('button[name="login"]').click(function() {
  var jid = $('input[name="jid"]').val()
  var password = $('input[name="password"]').val()
    if (!jid || !password) {
      return alert('Please enter connection details')
    }
    var options = { jid: jid, password: password }
    socket.send('xmpp.login', options)
})
```

Once you've completed this you can start up the server (using node index), open your browser to `http://localhost:3000/`, enter the JID `test@localhost` and the password `password`, and click on the `Login` button. Hopefully, we should see the connection status updated to read `Online`. Great stuff so far!

 Just in case you make an error in your code/outgoing data for events that don't have a callback function, it's also worth listening on the `xmpp.error.client` event so that you'll know if anything went wrong.

# Interacting with the chat bot

The next thing we're going to do is interact with the server-side chat bot we created earlier. To do this, we'll need to handle both sending and receiving a message, so we'll do this in two parts. To receive a message, in our xmpp.js file, we'll listen for a click on the **Send Message** button and output our message to the browser:

```
var sendMessage = function() {
  var message = $('textarea[name="outgoing-message"]').val()
  if (!message) return alert('Please enter a message!')
  var toSend = {
    to: 'bot@localhost' /* We'll hard code this for now */
    content: message
  }
var html = [ '<div class="message">', '<time>',
  new Date().toString(), '</time>', '<span >
  -&gt; </span> ', message, '</div>' ]
    $('div.received').append(html.join(''))
  socket.send('xmpp.chat.message', toSend)
}
$('button[name="send-message"]').click(sendMessage)
```

Easy right? Next, we'll handle receiving a chat message:

```
socket.on('xmpp.chat.message', receivedMessage)
var receivedMessage = function(incoming) {
 if (('localhost' !== incoming.from.domain) || ('bot' !==
incoming.from.local))
  {
    return /* Ignore messages from anywhere else */
  }
 if (!incoming.content) return
  /* Ignore anything which isn't a chat message */
  /* Note: We really should escape the message contents here! */
  var html = [ '<div class="message">', '<time>', new Date().toString(),
  '</time>', '<span > &lt;- </span> ',
    incoming.content, '</div>' ]
   $('div.received').append(html.join(''))
 }
```

Now we're handling incoming and outgoing messages from our bot. Should you wish to fire up the bot and refresh your browser, then after logging in, you should be able to send and receive messages. Super cool!

# Seeing what the chat bot is up to...

As we went through the effort of getting the chat bot to send chat state notifications, it would seem silly not to also display these to the end user so that they know that something is happening. To do this, we'll need to add another section of HTML and extend our received message function. In the HTML, we'll add a simple <p> tag after our received <div> to display the chat status, as follows:

```
<p class="chat-status"></p>
```

Next, we'll update the function call just above the if (!incoming.content) line to handle chat status notifications, making the function look like this:

```
var receivedMessage = function(incoming) {
   if (('localhost' !== incoming.from.domain) ||
('bot'!==incoming.from.local))
   {
     return /* Ignore messages from anywhere else */
   }
   handleChatState(incoming.state)
   if (!incoming.content) return
     /* Ignore anything which isn't a chat message */
     /* Note: We really should escape the message contents here! */
    var html = [ '<div class="message">', '<time>', new
    Date().toString(), '</time>', '<span >
    &lt;- </span> ', incoming.message.replace(/\n/g, '<br/>'), '</div>' ]
   $('div.received').append(html.join(''))
}
```

We can then implement the handleChatState method to, well, handle chat state updates. Remember, we only implemented a few of the states (active, inactive, and composing) in our bot, so we'll just handle these specifically:

```
var handleChatState = function(state) {
  if (!state) return /* Nothing to update */
  switch (state) {
    case 'active':  state = 'Reading question'; break
    case 'composing':
    default: state = 'Writing a response'; break
    case 'inactive': state = ''; break
  }
  $('p.chat-status').html(state)
}
```

Sweet! So now when our bot is off doing busy work, we'll see that it is busy serving our requests.

# Hello (hello, hello…)! Is there anybody out there?

Finally, it would be great to know if our bot was alive and kicking, or being lazy and taking a break from its duties and having a rest. To determine this information, we'll need to use `presence` and `presence subscriptions`. First, we'll update our code to tell the server that we're available on connection, make a `presence subscription` request to our bot (which it will automatically accept), and then display the presence of the bot on screen.

Let's add a little piece of HTML to `index.html` and default the bot to showing as offline (you just can't get the right bots sometimes!):

```
<p class="bot-status">Offline</p>
```

Now that we have this code in place, our first task is to send our own presence availability to the server once we've successfully logged in. We'll need to update the connected method to send our presence out:

```
var connected = function(details) {
  $('p.connection-status').html('Online')
  socket.send('xmpp.presence', { show: 'chat' })
}
```

Now we'll set up the code to listen for incoming presence status updates from the bot (remembering that the first time we run this code we won't actually have a subscription yet). Once again, we add code to our `xmpp.js` file:

```
socket.on('xmpp.presence', function(presence) {
  if (('localhost' !== presence.from.domain) || ('bot' !==
presence.from.local)) {
    return /* Ignore messages from anywhere else */
  }
var status = 'Offline'
switch (presence.show) {
  case 'chat': status = 'ready to answer!'; break
  case 'away':
  case 'xa':
    status = 'away.'; break
  case 'dnd': status = 'busy right now.': break
}
$('p.bot-status').html('Instant answer bot is ' + status)
})
```

The very final thing we'd need to do to get the XMPP server to send us presence updates for the bot is request a `presence subscription`. The way we'll do this is quite wasteful (since we're going to ask every page load regardless), but we can learn how to do this more efficiently later on. Let's jump back to our connected method and send out our presence subscription:

```
var connected = function(details) {
  $('p.connection-status').html('Online')
  socket.send('xmpp.presence', { show: 'chat' })
  socket.send('xmpp.presence.subscribe', { to: 'bot@localhost' })
}
```

That's it! Refresh your browser and start playing with the instant answer bot-like, asking it, "What is the best Pink Floyd song?" While you are at it, you should be able to stop and restart the bot node process and see its presence status change in real time in the browser.

# Summary

By the end of this chapter, we really starting to build some basic yet powerful stuff. With just presence, simple instant messaging, chat state, and a whole fleet of bots, we can already build quite powerful real time (and lets not forget federated) applications!

In this chapter, we learned about XMPP connection methods from the browser, we were introduced to and played with XMPP-FTW, we built a simple HTTP and WebSocket server to talk via the browser, and we built a browser-based client to chat with our instant answers bot from `Chapter 2`, *Diving into the Core XMPP Concepts*.

In the next chapter, we will build a **Multi-User Chat** (**MUC**) application with our newly gained knowledge of XMPP-FTW.

# 5
# Building a Multi-User Chat Application

To paraphrase a quote from a recent movie about a social network, "*One-to-one chats aren't cool. You know what's cool? Multiparty chats.*" And with that bold statement, we stride into the domain of Multi-User Chat (MUC).

In this chapter, we're going to learn the basics of multi-user chat rooms and how users are identified, discovered, and configured. Then we'll extend our bot to join a chat room and respond to messages. We will also build a simple browser-based MUC client using XMPP-FTW.

## The basics of MUC

At its most basic level, interacting with an MUC isn't that much different to holding a one-to-one conversation except that there are multiple parties (obviously!) and `<message/>` stanzas get a type of `groupchat` (or sometimes private). There's actually a bit more than that, but as soon as you understand this little bit of information, developing a multi-user chat will not be difficult.

## Joining a room

Let's take the example of Biff Tannen (`biff@tannen.hello`) and his gang hanging out at Lou's café, which we'll refer to as `gang@lous.cafe`.

Notice that a chat room address looks just like a JID! The MUC room itself will sit on a domain handled by an XMPP server and the `local` part becomes the identifier of the room itself, in this case, `gang`. This means that an MUC room is just a JID that you can talk to.

Now, joining a non-password-protected room is simple: no, wait! It's really simple. In essence, all we do is send a directed Presence (remember that from `Chapter 2`, *Diving into the Core XMPP Concepts*?) to the room we want to join with a chosen nickname (more on that later) and, provided it is not taken, we're in!

Let's say Marty turns up at the diner and wants to step into the conversation to help out George McFly:

```
<presence from='marty@mcfly.fam/diner'
id='join1'
to='gang@lous.cafe/calvin' />
```

Technically, we should also include a child element that signifies to the room that our XMPP client is able to speak XMPP MUC using a child tag, as follows:
`<x xmlns='http://jabber.org/protocol/muc'/>`.
But in practice, most XMPP servers are happy to continue without receiving this element.

In this example, Marty has requested to join the room we've already identified, but you'll notice that he has provided a full JID with the resource being the nickname he'd like to identify himself with, in this case, `Calvin`.

The room itself has a bare JID (`gang@lous.cafe`), but by appending Marty's room nickname, we have a full JID that allows us to address Marty directly which is `gang@lous.cafe/calvin`.

Upon joining a MUC, the server will start to fire a bunch of `<presence/>` stanzas at your client, giving you details about who is in the room (essentially a list of nicknames) and some information about their role within a room. This is referred to as the room's roster. Here's a quick example:

```
<!-- Marty joins the chat room -->
<presence from='marty@mcfly.fam/diner'
id='join1'
to='gang@lous.cafe/calvin' />

<!-- We receive an entry for Biff who is the room owner -->
<presence
from='gang@lous.cafe/biff'
id='roster1'
```

```
to='marty@mcfly.fam/diner'>
  <x xmlns='http://jabber.org/protocol/muc#user'>
    <item affiliation='owner' role='moderator'/>
  </x>
</presence>
<!-- We receive an entry for George who is a room member -->
<presence
    from='gang@lous.cafe/george'
    id='roster2'
    to='marty@mcfly.fam/diner'>
  <x xmlns='http://jabber.org/protocol/muc#user'>
    <item affiliation='member' role='participant'/>
  </x>
</presence>
<!-- We receive an entry for Skinhead who is a room admin -->
<presence
from='gang@lous.cafe/george'
id='roster3'
to='marty@mcfly.fam/diner'>
  <x xmlns='http://jabber.org/protocol/muc#user'>
    <item affiliation='admin' role='moderator'/>
  </x>
</presence>
```

While this is happening, each room member will also be sent a similar `<presence/>` stanza from Marty's room JID, informing them that someone new has joined (the actual affiliation and role would depend on the room configuration). For example:

```
<presence
from='gang@lous.cafe/calvin'
id='roster4'
to='biff@tannen.hello/lous'>
  <x xmlns='http://jabber.org/protocol/muc#user'>
    <item affiliation='member' role='participant'/>
  </x>
</presence>
```

# Your role and identity within a room

Now, something else to note is that within an MUC room, you are (mostly) anonymous. There is nothing to stop Marty from requesting to join with the nickname Calvin, Marty, or even Darth Vader.

MUCs can be set up such that none, a subset (such as the room owner or moderators), or all members can see your real JID, and this information can be found from the room configuration before joining. It is also possible to have a nickname reserved for a specific JID, or to request a nickname reservation. This ability is dependent on the XMPP service and whether the room owner has requested this feature.

For a room, a user has both a role and an affiliation (as we saw from the room roster stanzas). An affiliation is a permanent (well, for as long as the room exists) association that sticks with the user, while a user's role exists for their current session.

Allowed affiliation values are:

| Affiliation | Values |
|---|---|
| Owner | The room owner. He/She has full control over the room and its members. |
| Admin | A user who is able to administer (or moderate) the room and its members. |
| Member | A user with access to the room. |
| Outcast | A user who has been permanently banned from the room. |

The role values are as follows:

| Roles | Values |
|---|---|
| Moderator | A user who can administer the room and its members. |
| Participant | A user who can send a message to the room and potentially modify properties such as the room subject. However, this is controlled by the room configuration. |
| Visitor | A user with less access to the room than a participant, but they can still send and receive messages. The exact difference is determined by the room configuration. |

# Sending and receiving messages

Once you've joined a room, it is only natural to want to send and receive messages. Otherwise, why exactly would you have joined, right? Well, the good news is that if you can handle one-to-one chat messages, it is really rather simple to send and receive groupchat or even private messages.

If we remember our message stanzas from `Chapter 3`, *Building One-on-One Chat Bot – The "Hello World" of XMPP*, the `<message/>` element contained an attribute of type, which had a value of chat. Now, for multiuser chat, the value of type will be either `groupchat` for a message sent to everyone in the room or private for a message sent from one room occupant to yourself. Additionally, the message will come from the full room JID (that is, `room-name@domain/nickname`) rather than the actual user's JID.

For example, once Biff arrives at Lou's café (or our chat room version of it), he asks George for his homework assignment but he isn't worried about who sees his message. You will see from the following stanzas that all participants will receive Biff's message:

```
<!-- Biff sends a message to the room -->
<message type='groupchat'
from='biff@tannen.hello/lous'
to='gang@lous.cafe'>
  <body>
    ...and where are my reports?
  </body>
</message>
<!-- The message is then broadcast to everyone there -->
<message type='groupchat'
from='gang@lous.cafe/biff'
to='george@mcfly.fam/counter'>
  <body>
    ...and where are my reports?
  </body>
</message>
<message type='groupchat'
from='gang@lous.cafe/biff'
to='joey@skinhe.ad/lous'>
  <body>
    ...and where are my reports?
  </body>
</message>
```

If Biff had wanted to be more direct or discrete, he could have sent the message directly to George, so that no one else could see, by setting the *type* attribute to `private`:

```
<!-- Biff sends a message to the room -->
<message type='private'
from='biff@tannen.hello/lous'
to='gang@lous.cafe/george'>
  <body>
    ...and where are my reports?
  </body>
</message>
```

```
<!-- The message is then sent only to George McFly -->
<message type='private'
    from='gang@lous.cafe/biff'
    to='george@mcfly.fam/counter'>
  <body>
    ...and where are my reports?
  </body>
</message>
```

# Discovering MUC

Now we know all about joining and sending and receiving messages in a multiuser chat room, but one thing we haven't discussed so far is finding the darn things! Let's make that right.

As with most things in XMPP, if you as a user are trying to find out what things are there and what they do, you lean on your old friend DISCO. Let's look at a typical round trip to find an MUC room that we're interested in. First, we make a DISCO#info request to the server to see what features it supports:

```
<iq type='get' id='query1'
from='lorraine@baines.fam/dining-room'
to='chat.baines.fam'>
  <query xmlns='http://jabber.org/protocol/disco#info'/>
</iq>
```

The server will then return a list of features supported (note that this could potentially be a long list if the server supports a lot of features!):

```
<iq type='result' id='query1'
from='chat.baines.fam'
to='lorraine@baines.fam/dining-room'>
    <query xmlns='http://jabber.org/protocol/disco#info>
        <identity
          category='conference'
          name='Baines family conversations'
          type='text'/>
        <feature var='http://jabber.org/protocol/muc'/>
    </query>
</iq>
```

The XML namespace of `http://jabber.org/protocol/muc` identifies that this server provides a multiuser chat feature, so we can ask the server for a list of `items` (for example, available chat rooms) it holds:

```
<iq type='get' id='query2'
from='lorraine@baines.fam/dining-room'
to='chat.baines.fam'>
  <query xmlns='http://jabber.org/protocol/disco#items'/>
</iq>
```

The server will then return a list of chat rooms:

```
<iq type='result' id='query2'
from='chat.baines.fam'
to='lorraine@baines.fam/dining-room'>
    <query xmlns='http://jabber.org/protocol/disco#items'>
        <item jid='tv-dining@chat.baines.fam'/>
        <item jid='accident-victim@chat.baines.fam'/>
        <item jid='miltons-room@chat.baines.fam'/>
    </query>
</iq>
```

Lastly, we could query each of the rooms, with a `DISCO` info query to the room JID, to find out more:

```
<iq type='get' id='query3'
from='lorraine@baines.fam/dining-room'
to='tv-dining@chat.baines.fam'>
  <query xmlns='http://jabber.org/protocol/disco#info'/>
</iq>
<!-- ...with the response... -->
<iq type='result' id='query3'
from='tv-diningchat.baines.fam'
to='lorraine@baines.fam/dining-room'>
    <query xmlns='http://jabber.org/protocol/disco#info'>
        <identity
        category='conference'
        name='Food and TV in the same room!'
        type='text'/>
    <feature var='http://jabber.org/protocol/muc'/>
    <feature var='muc_unmoderated'/>
    <x xmlns='jabber:x:data' type='result'>
      <field var='FORM_TYPE' type='hidden'>
        <value>http://jabber.org/protocol/muc#roominfo</value>
      </field>
      <field var='muc#roominfo_description'
            label='Description'>
        <value>We now have TV in the dining room!</value>
```

```
        </field>
        <field var='muc#roominfo_contactjid'
               label='Contact Addresses'>
          <value>sam@baines.fam</value>
        </field>
        <field var='muc#roominfo_subject'
               label='Current Discussion Topic'>
          <value>Jackie Gleason is on!</value>
        </field>
      </x>
    </query>
  </iq>
```

In the response, you'll note that the `entity` once again identifies itself as a multiuser chat room and also advertises some features that it supports, such as the fact that it is unmoderated. Lastly, the response includes a data form (which we're about to get on to) that gives the curious investigator more details about the properties and configuration of the room itself.

Here we went straight to `chat.baines.fam` to perform our initial DISCO info request. In reality, we wouldn't know what domains are available for an XMPP server (especially a remote one!), and so we would first need to perform a DISCO items query on the server. This would return a list of items we could inspect, much as we did when we inspected the chat room itself. We'll probably find that our MUC service is running using its own component. While this is not a slow process, clients should cache some results to make discovery faster with later requests and to provide a better user experience.

# Configuring our chat room using data forms

At some point, we will want to configure our chat room to do different things, for example, only allow new users to read the messages, maybe add a password, or just set the room name. While this may seem feasible to handle custom stanzas for a few of these types of changes, when you expand to all the use cases just for configuration, then learning/knowing all of these systems would become a nightmare.

Thankfully, XMPP provides something called a data form; it can help address this dilemma. Data forms (as defined in **XEP-0004**) provide a standard way of requesting and setting structured data. They can be thought of as analogous to forms on a web page, and indeed you may notice several similarities.

# The basics of the data form

You'll be able to identify a data form by its distinctive opening tag:

```
<x xmlns='jabber:x:data'>
```

Once we see a tag like this, we'll know that we're working with a data form and we can act accordingly. Data forms are broken into a set of fields, each described by a variable and a type. Moreover, the form can have a title and instructions as well as a couple of additional elements used for reporting results (but let's not worry about that for a moment).

The form itself will also have a type, which is set depending on how it is being used:

| Type | Description |
|--------|-------------|
| form | To request a data form, for example, what parameters can I configure |
| submit | To submit data to the delivering entity, for example, setting room configurations |
| cancel | This is used when we want to cancel a request, for example, part way through a multi-stage process |
| result | The result returned from the server, for example, the chat room describing what parameters can be configured |

Next, let's take a look at a very simple data form. Picture the scene: George McFly is in a conversation with Biff and his gang at Lou's café (our chat room), but so far he hasn't been allowed to speak (he's a visitor in the conversation). He now wants to say something (that is, become a participant), so he requests permission to speak:

```
<message from='george@mcfly.fam/counter'
id='request1'
to='gang@lous.cafe'>
  <x xmlns='jabber:x:data' type='submit'>
    <field var='FORM_TYPE'
          type='hidden'>
      <value>http://jabber.org/protocol/muc#request</value>
    </field>
    <field var='muc#role'
          type='text-single'
          label='Requested role'>
      <value>participant</value>
    </field>
  </x>
</message>
```

As you can see, this is a very simple form with two fields. However, forms can contain as many fields as required. The first field represents the form type (var ='FORM_TYPE') and is marked as hidden, as it is used to identify the form on return to the sender but it is not really of interest to the user. The second field is of type text-single, which represents a single line of text, much like the `<input type='text'/>` element in HTML. You'll note that the `muc#role` field also contains a label attribute, which is a human-readable string representing the data that the form element represents. Below this, we have a value element, which contains the form field value. If this were a type where multiple entries could be contained, then we could include multiple value children.

There are several data types that can be contained within a data form field:

| Data Types | Description |
| --- | --- |
| **boolean** | Represents a true or false value, similar to `<input type='checkbox'/>` in HTML. Both true (or 1) and false (or 0) are valid values for this field type. |
| **fixed** | A form field that is displayed to the user but isn't editable in any way. |
| **hidden** | A form field that should not be displayed to the user and generally is not edited (for example, it may be used to carry some sort of state in a multipart form). Compare this with `<input type='hidden'/>` in HTML. |
| **list-multi** | A field that allows the user to select multiple values from a list of possible options, similar to `<select/>` in HTML but with the multiple attribute set. Note that there is A specialized version of this with type jid-multi, which allows the user to pick multiple JIDs in a list. |
| **list-single** | Much like list-multi except that the user can only select a single option from the list, and consequently is like an unmodified `<select/>` HTML form element. Additionally, there is jid-single, which allows the user to pick a single JID from a set of options. |
| **text-multi** | Analogous to a `<textarea/>`, this allows the user to enter multiple lines of text, but with a key difference; each new line is stored in its own `<value/>` element. |
| **text-private** | This field type allows a user to enter a single line of text, but the data contained is masked, similar in style to an HTML password input (that is, `<input type='password'/>`). |
| **text-single** | Lastly, this field type allows for a single line of text entry from the user, much like a standard input in an HTML form field (for example, `<input type='text'/>`). |

# Getting our MUC room configuration

Now that we know the basics, let's work through the process of getting and updating a chat room configuration with a real example. First, we need to obtain the existing room configuration along with the configuration form itself. As Biff is the owner of the chat room, he makes the get request:

```
<iq from='biff@tannen.hello/lous'
id='configuration-1'
type='get'
to='gang@lous.cafe'>
  <query xmlns='http://jabber.org/protocol/muc#owner'/>
</iq>
```

The server then returns to him a list of the configurable options as well as their current value(s) if set:

```
<iq from='gang@lous.cafe'
id='configuration-1'
to='biff@tannen.hello/lous'
type='result'>
  <query xmlns='http://jabber.org/protocol/muc#owner'>
    <x xmlns='jabber:x:data' type='form'>
      <title>Configuration for "gang" Room</title>
      <instructions>
        Update this form to modify the configuration of the chat room
      </instructions>
      <field
          type='hidden'
          var='FORM_TYPE'>
        <value>http://jabber.org/protocol/muc#roomconfig</value>
      </field>
      <field
          label='Room Name'
          type='text-single'
          var='muc#roomconfig_roomname'>
        <value>Biff's gang @ the diner</value>
      </field>
      <field
          label='Maximum Number of Users'
          type='list-single'
          var='muc#roomconfig_maxusers'>
      <value>5</value>
      <option label='5'><value>5</value></option>
      <option label='10'><value>10</value></option>
      <option label='15'><value>15</value></option>
      </field>
```

```
            <field
                label='Members Only?'
                type='boolean'
                var='muc#roomconfig_membersonly'>
              <value>1</value>
            </field>
            <field type='fixed'>
              <value>
                Specify additional owners for this
                room, providing one JID per line.
              </value>
            </field>
            <field
                label='Room Owners'
                type='jid-multi'
                var='muc#roomconfig_roomowners'/>
        </x>
    </query>
</iq>
```

In this example, we have a very small number of fields, but in reality the list could be much larger.

> If a mere participant such as Marty McFly were to request the room configuration using the XML namespace `http://jabber.org/protocol/muc#owner`, he would simply receive an error response. To determine a configuration for non-moderators, we would use a `DISCO` info request as we learned earlier.

# Updating the room configuration

Now that Biff knows the current room configuration, he can either decide to cancel his request or update the settings. To cancel his request, he would simply send an empty form of type cancel. But if he wants to update the room configuration, he can do something like this:

```
<iq from='biff@tannen.hello/lous'
id='update-config-1'
to='gang@lous.cafe'
type='set'>
    <query xmlns='http://jabber.org/protocol/muc#owner'>
      <x xmlns='jabber:x:data' type='submit'>
        <field
            type='hidden'
            var='FORM_TYPE'>
```

```
            <value>http://jabber.org/protocol/muc#roomconfig</value>
        </field>
        <field
            label='Room Name'
            type='text-single'
            var='muc#roomconfig_roomname'>
        <value>Biff's Cool Gang</value>
        </field>
        <field
            label='Maximum Number of Users'
            type='list-single'
            var='muc#roomconfig_maxusers'>
        <value>5</value>
        </field>
      <field
            label='Members Only?'
            type='boolean'
            var='muc#roomconfig_membersonly'>
        <value>1</value>
        </field>
        <field
            label='Room Owners'
            type='jid-multi'
            var='muc#roomconfig_roomowners'>
            <value>biff@tannen.hello</value>
            <value>joey@skinhe.ad</value>
        </field>
    </x>
  </query>
</iq>
```

Here, you'll notice that we can leave out much of the additional data when being told about the configuration options and existing values, but we must include FORM_TYPE so that the server is able to identify the form and its purpose.

On successfully updating the room configuration, the server would respond with a result IQ stanza so that Biff knows his updates were successfully made:

```
<iq from='gang@lous.cafe'
id='update-config-1'
to='biff@tannen.hello/lous'
type='result' />
```

# Data forms in XMPP-FTW

As data forms follow a set format, they are easy to map to and from JSON for use with XMPP-FTW. The only minor difference with data forms is that as we are using named events, XMPP-FTW is able to fill in the FORM_TYPE on your behalf; so it's a little simpler again.

If we take the preceding example in which we configured a chat room, we'd have the following in XMPP-FTW:

```
socket.send(
  'xmpp.muc.room.config.get',
  { "room": "gang@lous.cafe" },
  function(error, data) { console.log(error, data) }
)
```

The server would then respond with a data form formatted, like so:

```
{
  title: "Configuration for "gang" Room",
  instructions: "Update this form to modify the configuration of the chat
  room", fields: [
    { var: "muc#roomconfig_roomname", type: "text-single", required: false,
     value: "Biff's gang @ the diner", label: "Room Name" },
    {
      var: "muc#roomconfig_maxusers",
      type: "list-single",
      required: false,
      value: '5',
      label: "Maximum Number of Users",
      options: [
        { label: '5', value: '5' },
        { label: '10', value: '10' },
        { label: '15', value: '15' }
      ]
    },
    {
      var: "muc#roomconfig_membersonly",
      type: "boolean",
      required: false,
      value: true,
      label: "Members Only?"
    },
    {
      type: "fixed",
      required: false,
      value: 'Specify additional owners for this room, providing one JID
      per line.'
```

```
    },
    {
        var: "muc#roomconfig_roomowners",
        type: "jid-multi",
        required: false,
        label: "Room Owners"
    }
  ]
}
```

> Wherever we have data forms mixed in with other elements, it is a convention to hold the data form under a `form` key when both sending and receiving the fields. A full description can be found at `http://xmpp-ftw.jit.su/manual/data-forms/`.

Using much the same format as the sent form, you would now respond as follows:

```
var form = [
  { var: "muc#roomconfig_roomname", value: "Biff's Cool Gang" },
  { var: "muc#roomconfig_maxusers", value: '5' },
  { var: "muc#roomconfig_membersonly", value: true },
  { var: "muc#roomconfig_roomowners", value: [ 'biff@tannen.hello',
    'joey@skinhe.ad' ] }
]
socket.send(
  'xmpp.muc.room.config.set',
  { "room": "gang@lous.cafe", "form":  form },
  function(error, success) { console.log(error, success) }
)
```

Having requested to update the form, our callback would then be triggered with a null value for error and a true for success.

# Creating a chat room

Of course, before we can ever configure our chat room we must first have created one. There are two types of room: an instant room and a reserved room. An instant room is created by the owner and it immediately allows others to join and start chatting. A reserved room is created and locked until configured by the owner.

The initial stages of creating a room are exactly the same with the creator (who becomes the owner) sending a presence stanza to the JID of the room they wish to create. So let's continue with our above example and say Biff would like to create the gang chat room at Lou's café:

```
<presence from='biff@tannen.hello/lous'
to='gang@lous.cafe/biff'>
<x xmlns='http://jabber.org/protocol/muc'/>
</presence>
```

The server could respond in a couple of ways, but let's imagine a first example that Biff would not be very pleased with:

```
<presence from='gang@lous.cafe/biff'
to='biff@tannen.hello/lous'>
  <error by='gang@lous.cafe' type='cancel'>
    <not-allowed xmlns='urn:ietf:params:xml:ns:xmpp-stanzas'/>
  </error>
</presence>
```

In this case, the chat service is letting Biff know that he's not allowed to create the chat room. This might occur if, for example, the chat room already exists.

Now let's say Biff had been a good boy and was allowed to create his new chat room. The server would send a response as follows:

```
<presence from='gant@lous.cafe/biff'
to='biff@tannen.hello/lous'>
  <x xmlns='http://jabber.org/protocol/muc#user'>
    <item affiliation='owner' role='moderator'/>
      <status code='110'/>
      <status code='201'/>
  </x>
</presence>
```

What this says to Biff is that the room was successfully created and he has been made the owner with the role of room moderator, which I'm sure makes Biff very happy! The additional status elements are informational; with a status of 110, meaning that this presence update refers to him, and 201 which informs him that the room has just been created, but more on status numbers later!

At this point, the room is still locked to the rest of the gang and Biff now has to decide how he wants to proceed. If he'd like to accept the server defaults for the new room and start allowing Match, Skinhead, and 3-D to join the room immediately he could send an empty configuration stanza to the room, accepting the defaults, and opening it up:

```
<iq from='biff@tannen.hello/lous'
to='gang@lous.cafe/biff'
id='open-says-me'
type='set'>
  <query xmlns='http://jabber.org/protocol/muc#owner'>
    <x xmlns='jabber:x:data' type='submit'/>
  </query>
</iq>
```

If, however, Biff would like to configure the room before it is opened up to the rest of the gang for example, to add a password or set the room description then he can go through the room configuration stages as we went through them in the last section, starting with a request for the configuration form:

```
<iq from='biff@tannen.hello/lous'
to='gang@lous.cafe/biff'
id='configure-room-1'
type='get'>
    <query xmlns='http://jabber.org/protocol/muc#owner'/>
</iq>
```

Once Biff configures the gang's cool new chat room and its accepted by the server, the room is then opened up for the other members to join.

# Managing the users

The next thing Biff may want to do is to control/organize/manage (/bully?) the other participants in the chat room. There are two things he can do here:

- Change their role (session-length association to the chat room)
- Change their affiliation (permanent association to the chat room)

These requests are made using an `iq` stanza to which the room sends a result. The subject of the association change is then informed through a presence stanza and then the rest of the room is also informed via presence stanzas.

Let's say that Biff doesn't want George McFly talking back to him within his gang's conversation. Let's see how he'd go about making George silent (or revoking his voice). First, Biff requests a list of people in the chat who have the ability to speak (that is, they have the role of participant):

```
<iq from='biff@tannen.hello/lous'
to='gang@lous.cafe'
id='user-list'
type='set'>
  <query xmlns='http://jabber.org/protocol/muc#admin'>
    <item role='participant'/>
  </query>
</iq>
```

The room then responds to Biff with a list of current occupants:

```
<iq from='gang@lous.cafe'
to='biff@tannen.hello/lous'
id='user-list'
type='result'>
  <query xmlns='http://jabber.org/protocol/muc#admin'>
    <item affiliation='member'
      jid='joey@skinhe.ad/lous'
      nick='skinhead'
      role='participant'/>
    <item affiliation='member'
      jid='george@mcfly.fam/counter'
      nick='george'
      role='participant'/>
    <!-- Marty isn't yet part of the conversation -->
    <item affiliation='none'
      jid='marty@mcfly.fam/diner'
      nick='calvin'
      role='participant'/>
  </query>
</iq>
```

Biff sees that George is part of the conversation and is able to speak so he tells the room that he wants to silence George (and includes an optional reason):

```
<iq from='biff@tannen.hello/lous'
to='gang@lous.cafe'
id='be-quiet'
type='set'>
  <query xmlns='http://jabber.org/protocol/muc#admin'>
    <item nick='george' role='visitor'>
      <reason>Hey, shut up McFly!</reason>
    </item>
```

```
    </query>
  </iq>
```

The room then responds that the request was successful (with an IQ type result stanza) and then proceeds to inform George and the other gang members of the change:

```
<!-- Update sent to George -->
<presence from='gang@lous.cafe'
to='george@mcfly.fam/counter'>
  <x xmlns='http://jabber.org/protocol/muc#user'>
    <item affiliation='member'
      nick='george'
      role='visitor'>
      <reason>Hey, shut up McFly!</reason>
    </item>
  </x>
</presence>
<!-- Update sent to Skinhead -->
    <presence from='gang@lous.cafe'
    to='joey@skinhe.ad/lous'>
    <x xmlns='http://jabber.org/protocol/muc#user'>
      <item affiliation='member'
        nick='george'
        role='visitor' />
    </x>
</presence>
```

# Configuration updates

In the preceding data forms section, we saw how to change a room configuration. The room owner(s) can change the room configuration at any time when the room is in existence. The server is obliged to update the occupants about any changes that affect the security or privacy of their room membership. This is achieved by pushing out a message stanza to each occupant with a status code summarizing the change. For example:

```
<message from='gang@lous.cafe'
to='joey@skinhe.ad/lous'>
  <x xmlns='http://jabber.org/protocol/muc#user'>
    <status code='173' />
  </x>
</message>
```

In this example, the room is informing Skinhead that the room is now semi-anonymous. Status codes are used throughout MUC updates (mainly for legacy reasons) and are used to convey a whole range of quick information. These are summarized in this table:

| Status | Stanza type | Related to | Description |
|---|---|---|---|
| 100 | `<message/>` | Entering a room | Lets the user know that anyone can see their real JID |
| 101 | `<message/>` while not active in the chat room | Affiliation changes | While the user is not in the room, it lets the user know that their affiliation has changed |
| 102 | `<message/>` | Configuration changes | The occupant list now shows unavailable members |
| 103 | `<message/>` | Configuration changes | The occupant list does not show unavailable members |
| 104 | `<message/>` | Configuration changes | Lets the users know there has been a non-privacy/security related configuration change |
| 110 | `<presence/>` | Any presence change | Lets the user know that the presence change refers to themselves |
| 170 | `<message/>` or initial `<presence/>` | Configuration changes | The room is now being logged |
| 171 | `<message/>` | Configuration changes | The room is not being logged |
| 172 | `<message/>` | Configuration changes | The room is not anonymous (other users can see their real JID) |
| 173 | `<message/>` | Configuration changes | The room is now semi-anonymous |
| 174 | `<message/>` | Configuration change | The room is now fully-anonymous |
| 201 | `<presence/>` | Entering a room | A new room has been created |
| 210 | `<presence/>` | Entering a room | The room has set or changed the occupant's nickname |
| 301 | `<presence/>` | Removal from room | The user has been banned from the room |

| 303 | `<presence/>` | Leaving a room | Lets all users know about a new nickname |
|-----|---------------|----------------|------------------------------------------|
| 307 | `<presence/>` | Leaving a room | Lets the user know that they have been banned |
| 321 | `<presence/>` | Leaving a room | The user is leaving the room because of an affiliation change |
| 322 | `<presence/>` | Leaving a room | The user is being removed as the room is no-members-only and they are not a member |
| 332 | `<presence/>` | Leaving a room | The server is shutting down, so they are being removed from the room |

# Leaving a room

To leave a room, much like going offline, a user simply sends a presence stanza to the room of type unavailable. This removes them from the room and updates other occupants that they have left:

```
<!-- Marty - aka Calvin - decides to leave the chat -->
<presence from='gang@lous.cafe/calvin'
  to='joey@skinhe.ad/lous' type='unavailable'/>
<!-- Others in the room are informed -->
<presence from='gang@lous.cafe/calvin'
  to='joey@skinhe.ad/lous' type='unavailable'/>
<presence from='gang@lous.cafe/calvin'
    to='biff@tannen.hello/lous' type='unavailable'/>
```

# Destroying the room

Ultimately, the owner of a room may wish to remove it completely from the server. This can easily be done by sending the appropriate stanza:

```
<iq from='biff@tannen.hello/lous'
to='gang@lous.cafe'
id='be-quiet'
type='set'>
  <query xmlns='http://jabber.org/protocol/muc#owner'>
    <destroy jid='highschool@hill.valley'>
      <reason>Let's make like a tree, and get out of here!</reason>
    </destroy>
  </query> </iq>
```

In this case, Biff has decided to destroy the chat his gang were having in the cafe and suggested that everyone heads to a new chat room, (optionally specified) `highschool@hill.valley`, with his own version of let's get out of here!

Once he's sent the command to destroy the room, each member of the gang will receive a presence message informing them that the room is gone, Biff's suggested new location, and his reason for getting rid of the chat room:

```
<presence from='gang@lous.cafe/calvin'
to='joey@skinhe.ad/lous' type='unavailable'>
    <x xmlns='http://jabber.org/protocol/muc#user'>
      <item affiliation='none' role='none'/>
        <destroy jid='highschool@hill.valley'>
          <reason>Let's make like a tree, and get out of here!</reason>
        </destroy>
    </x>
</presence>
```

Once all the current occupants are informed of the room deletion, the server will let Biff know that the room has been destroyed successfully with a result stanza:

```
<iq from='gang@lous.cafe' to='biff@tannen.hello/lous'
    id='be-quiet' type='result'/>
```

# Building with XMPPMUC

Now, that we've been through the basics of multiuser chat operation, it is time we did something practical, so limber up your fingers and let's get coding! In the next two sections, we're going to update the configuration of our XMPP server to support MUC, extend our chat bot to work with an MUC, and build a simple chat system for a website that will allow anonymous visitors to communicate with each other. Sounds fun! Let's go…

# Updating Prosody to provide an MUC service

Many XMPP servers come with their own MUC implementations that make it easy to get a chat service up and running and you'll be glad to hear that Prosody is no exception. In fact, it's no more than one additional line of configuration to get it up and running.

Fire up your terminal and let's edit the Prosody configuration file (in Ubuntu which can be found at `/etc/prosody/prosody.cfg.lua`) at the bottom of the file, we'll add a single line:

```
Component "chat.localhost" "muc"
```

Once you've saved the file, restart Prosody. And we'll have a chat service up and running at `chat.localhost`.

There are actually very few options to set for a chat room, since each room can be heavily customized using configuration. The three additional options that Prosody MUC will support are:

| Option | Options / Example values | Description |
| --- | --- | --- |
| name | For example, "XMPP Chat rooms" | When an XMPP entity performs a `DISCO#info` on the component, this is what it will report as its name. |
| restrict_room_creation | true/false/local | If this is true, rooms can only be created by users in the 'admins' section. By specifying 'local', only users on the same domain (or parent domain) will be able to create a room. |
| max_history_messages | For example, 20 | The maximum number of history messages a user can retrieve on joining a room. |

A full configuration therefore could look something like:

```
Component "chat.localhost" "muc"
  name = "Back to the Future chatrooms"
  restrict_room_creation = true
  max_history_messages = 50
```

# Connecting with our XMPP client

The next thing we'll do is create a chat room using our XMPP client and just post a couple of messages (because, why not!).

We pop open our copy of **Empathy** and visit the main menu. We navigate to **Room** and then click on **Join Rooms**. This presents us with a dialog where we'll be able to create our chat room. Give your room a name and enter the server as `chat.localhost`, which is the domain we setup in Prosody a moment ago:

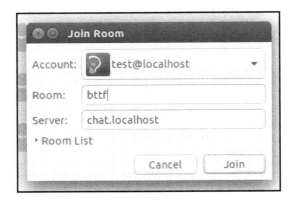

Next, click on **Join** and... hey presto! We have our first chat room! Now you should have a chat window pop up where you can start posting messages to the room:

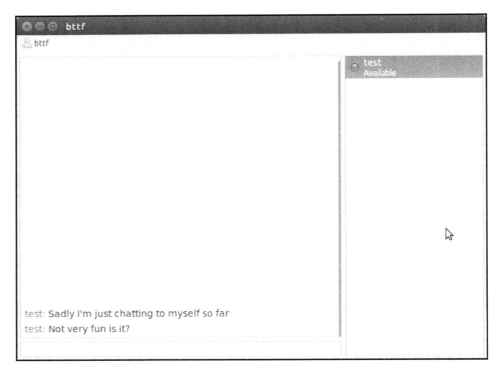

Interestingly, if you now pop back to the Join menu option, once again enter the server as `chat.localhost` but now open the room list option. You'll see our new room is listed. This will have been found by performing a `DISCO#items` request against the server domain; we'll do this ourselves later on.

# Extending our chat bot to work with an MUC

The next thing we're going to do is extend our chat bot to connect to the MUC room so that it can respond to group messages and private messages as well as continue to respond to one-to-one chat messages.

Now, as we know, MUC messages simply involve a change in type from chat to groupchat (or messages remain as chat but are delivered from an MUC JID in the case of a private message), so responding to messages should be easy. If receiving a group chat message, we'll probably want to add the sender's nickname in the response so that they know it's a response to them (most clients will flag a mention of the user's nickname to them) and only respond to queries that mention the bot's nickname. The only other task we then need to perform is joining the chat room in the first place.

The first thing we'll do is add another method call when the bot detects that it is online, and then send out a presence stanza in order to join the room:

```
client.on('online', (connectionDetails) => {
  ... existing code ...
  joinChatRoom()
})

const joinChatRoom = () => {
  const stanza = new ltx.Element(
    'presence',
    { to: 'bttf@chat.localhost/answer-bot' }
  )
  console.log('Joining chat room: ' + stanza.toString())
  client.send(stanza)
}
```

 As we're limited for space, we're not handling errors (such as refusal to join, room not existing, nickname taken, and so on) but this is something you'd want to do in a robust system.

Next we need to handle responding to messages. This falls under five tasks:

- Add the appropriate type attribute value to our response
- If it is a `groupchat` type message, include the sender's nickname in the response
- If it is a `groupchat` message or a private MUC message, then we shouldn't send chat state notifications
- If it is a `groupchat` type message, we should send the response to the room JID and not the member's room JID (essentially we'd want to remove `/nickname`)
- If the message is from a chat room, only respond if the message mentions the bot's nickname (since we don't want to respond to every message as if it's a query)

The easiest way to detect if a message of type chat is a private MUC message is to compare the start of the sender JID with our known chat room JID. If they match, then it's an MUC message and chat state notifications should not be sent:

```
const isMessageFromChatRoom = (0 ===
stanza.attr('from').indexOf('bttf@chat.localhost'))
const sendChatStateNotifications = (
  ('groupchat' !== stanza.attr('type'))
  && !isMessageFromChatRoom)
)
```

We also want to prefix all our responses with the sender's nickname if it's a `groupchat` message, so let's write some code for that:

```
let responsePrefix = ''
if (isMessageFromChatRoom && ('groupchat' === stanza.attr('type')))
{
  const jid = new Client.JID(stanza.attr('from'))
  responsePrefix = jid.getResource() + ': '
}
```

If the message is of type `groupchat`, we also need to update the `to` address of the stanza to the room JID (and not the sender's full room JID):

```
if ('groupchat' === stanza.attr('type')) {
  const jid = new Client.JID(stanza.attr('from'))
  const from = jid.bare()
}
```

Lastly, for new bits of code, we only want to respond to a `groupchat` if it's directed at our bot:

```
if ('groupchat' === stanza.attr('type')) {
  if (0 !== query.indexOf('answer-bot:'))) {
    return /* Not for us to respond to */
  }
  query = query.replace('answer-bot: ', '')
}
```

Now we can pick up our `handleMessage` function from `Chapter 3`, *Building One-on-One Chat Bot – The "Hello World" of XMPP* and add our new bits of code so that our bot will respond to MUC messages too (edited to make use of defined variables):

```
const handleMessage = function(stanza) {
  let query = stanza.getChildText('body')
  if (!query) return /* Not a chat message */
  const from = stanza.attr('from')
  const type = stanza.attr('type')
  const isMessageFromChatRoom = (0 ===
from.indexOf('bttf@chat.localhost'))
  const sendChatStateNotifications = (
    ('groupchat' !== type) && !isMessageFromChatRoom
  )
  if ('groupchat' === type) {
    if (0 !== query.indexOf('answer-bot:')) {
      return /* Not for us to respond to */
    }
    query = query.replace('answer-bot: ', '')
```

```
    }
    if (sendChatStateNotifications) sendChatState(from, 'active')
    ddg.query(query, function(error, data) {
      if (sendChatStateNotifications) sendChatState(from, 'composing')
      const result = null
      if (error) {
        result = 'Unfortunately we could not answer your request'
      } else {
        if (!data.RelatedTopics[0]) {
          result = 'Sorry, there were no results!'
        } else const {
          const item = data.RelatedTopics[0]
          result = item.FirstURL + '\n' + item.Text
        }
      }
      let responsePrefix = ''
      if (isMessageFromChatRoom && ('groupchat' === type)) {
        const jid = new Client.JID(from)
        responsePrefix = jid.getResource() + ': '
        from = jid.bare()
      }
      const reply = new ltx.Element(
        'message',
        { type: 'chat', to: from }
      )
      reply.c('body').t(responsePrefix + result)
      if (sendChatStateNotifications) {
        reply.c('inactive', { xmlns: NS_CHAT_STATE })
      }
      console.log('Sending response: ' + reply.root().toString())
      client.send(reply)
    })
}
```

Now that we're done, we can use our client to interact with the chat bot. Firing up the script, we see that the bot joins the chat room and responds to MUC messages too:

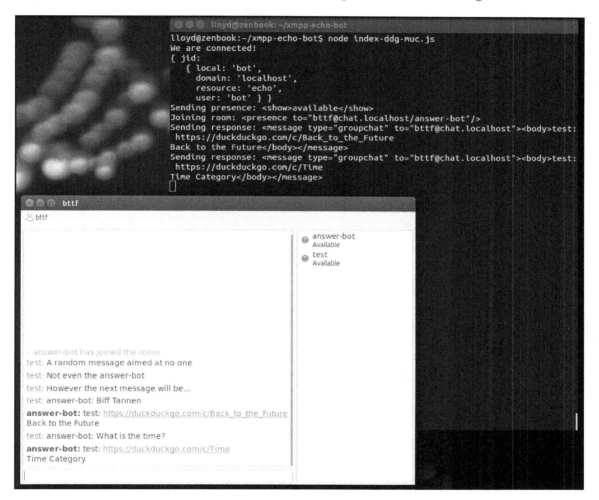

Congratulations! You've now created the basis of a very powerful bot. Imagine how you can extend this bot to make your team more effective. By having a bot, you can make requests such as run the build or release the software and help everyone in your team be aware.

Once you have a setup like this, the possibilities are endless and are only limited by language conversations between people. Why can't bots interact with other bots to run much larger processes requiring collaboration?

# Writing a browser-based MUC client

In this last section, we're doing to write something more exciting that will allow visitors to visit a website, view a list of chat rooms, choose to enter one, and then interact with other users in realtime. They'll also be able to see a list of other members in the room and get notifications of when they leave and new ones join.

To keep things simple (well, enough for a book), we're not going to cover password-protected rooms, changes in affiliation/role (everyone will be able to write), private messages, invites, and a whole bunch of other stuff, but we will cover joining errors so that we can ensure our users get to chat!

But won't users need XMPP accounts? One thing you might have realized is: without usernames and passwords, how are users meant to connect to the server and join in the conversations? Well, there are two options here:

1. Allow users to sign up as they connect, also known as in-band registration. This isn't the best solution since it opens up your servers to spammers, who will create accounts and fire off messages, possibly getting your server banned from S2S connections with other XMPP servers (see `Chapter 10`, *Real-world Deployment and XMPP Extensions* for more details).
2. Make use of SASL's anonymous authentication mechanism (defined in `https://tools.ietf.org/html/rfc4505`), which allows users to connect without first creating an account. Generally, you'd ban anonymous users from S2S communications, limiting their ability to cause mischief. In this example code, we're going to make use of ANONYMOUS authentication since it simplifies things, and as users are connecting for short chat sessions, there's no need for them to own an account on your server.

# Setting things up server-side

First, to prevent abuse by users, we'll update our XMPP server configuration to support anonymous authentication (which we'll do on its own special domain). By default, Prosody will block anonymous users from making S2S calls unless specifically allowed, which saves us some extra configuration.

Open up your Prosody configuration file and add the following virtual host using an anonymous authentication:

```
VirtualHost "anonymous.localhost"
    authentication = "anonymous"
```

After restarting Prosody, we'll be able to make anonymous connections to the server.

As we don't have DNS setup, we'll add a quick hint in our hosts file to ensure that our xmpp-ftw server knows where to look for the new anonymous domain:

```
sudo vim /etc/hosts
# add the following line to the file
127.0.0.1 anonymous.localhost
```

Next, we're once again going to start from the xmpp-ftw skeleton project as a base and then make some updates to restrict the functionality that anonymous users can make use of via our website:

```
cd ~
git clone git@github.com:xmpp-ftw/skeleton-project.gitmuc-example
cd muc-example
```

This time, before installing all the project dependencies, we're going to make a small change to the package.json file and add a couple of more dependencies. Open the file and remove the line under dependencies for xmpp-ftw-buddycloud (since we're not going to be using that module in this project). Once saved, we can install our dependencies and an additional couple of xmpp-ftw modules:

```
npm i .
npm i --save xmpp-ftw-muc xmpp-ftw-disco
```

As you may have guessed, one of the added modules is for handling MUC functionality, with the other adding support for DISCO queries.

Next we'll set up the last of the server-side code before we head directly to building the fun part! In index.js, we're going to remove the default listeners (presence, chat, and roster) and inject the DISCO and MUC listeners instead, reducing the functionality that users have access to via the browser. Open your new project's index.js file, and where we see the listener for the connection event, we'll update the code to read:

```
primus.on('connection', (socket) => {
  console.log('Websocket connection made')
  const xmppFtw = new xmpp.Xmpp(socket)
  xmppFtw.clearListeners()
  xmppFtw.addListener(new Disco())
  xmppFtw.addListener(new Muc())
  socket.xmppFtw = xmppFtw
})
```

Before we start the code, we have to import the two required modules and then we're done. So in the same file near the top, we need to remove this line:

```
, Buddycloud = require('xmpp-ftw-buddycloud')
```

And add the following two instead:

```
, Disco = require('xmpp-ftw-disco')
, Muc = require('xmpp-ftw-muc')
```

OK, great! Now we have an XMPP server capable of handling anonymous sessions and an xmpp-ftw setup that provides us with just enough functionality to build our application.

# Building the client

When building the client, there are three files we'll be editing; let's quickly list these to make referencing them later much easier:

- views/index.ejs: The HTML that will be delivered by our server to the browser. It loads the page structure, the JavaScript, and the required CSS. We'll refer to this as the HTML file.

- `public/css/style.css`: The style file where we'll put all our CSS declarations, the style (or CSS) file.
- `public/scripts/xmpp.js`: The file where we'll put all our JavaScript for the client, our JavaScript file.

We'll build these files slowly so that each part is understood as we go along.

# Connecting anonymously

The first thing we should do is remove all the unnecessary functions within our JavaScript file, so delete the following functions:

- `handleItems`
- `getNodeItems`
- `discoverBuddycloudServer`

The great thing is that the skeleton project already has an anonymous login setup in place for us, so we can just edit it to match our requirements. The login function should look like this:

```
var login = function() {
  socket.send(
    'xmpp.login.anonymous',
      { jid: '@anonymous.localhost' }
  )
  socket.on('xmpp.connection', function(data) {
    console.log('Connected as', data.jid)
  })
}
```

If we now start up the server and open our browser in the developer console (*F12* should make it appear, if you aren't familiar), we should discover that we are connected anonymously:

```
node index.js
```

Now open the browser and open `http://localhost:3000`

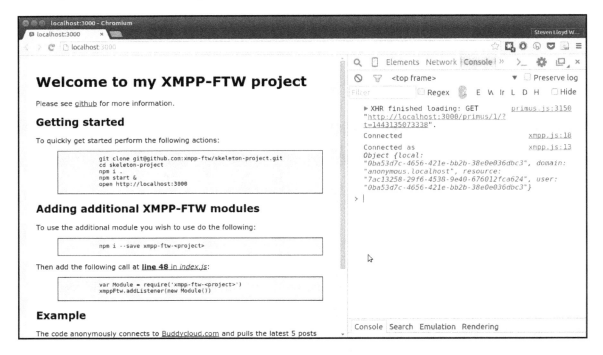

As you can see from the image, Prosody has assigned us a long, random JID on the `anonymous.localhost` domain. Hopefully, you are seeing something very similar in your console.

From this point, we can leave the `xmpp-ftw` server running and just edit the three files mentioned previously to achieve our goals.

# Listing the available chat rooms

Our next task is to list the chat rooms that are available on the server for the user to join. We'll probably want to set up some HTML so that the user can see the list. We can populate the list once the details come in using JavaScript. So let's put some outline HTML in place. Open your HTML file and change the content between the `<body/>` tags to the following:

```
<section id="room-list">
  <h1>Chat room system</h1>
  <h2>Choose a chat room to join</h2>
  <ul class="js-chat-room-list">
```

```
    <li>Loading chat room list</li>
  </ul>
  <h2>Choose a nickname</h2>
  <input name="nick" required="true"
    placeholder="Enter nickname here" />
    <button type="button">Join room</button>
</section>
```

In this HTML file, we've defined three separate pieces: a list to hold our list of available chat rooms, a textbox where the user can enter their desired nickname, and a button to allow the user to join the chat room. We'll probably want to style these, so let's update our style file (style.css) to make things look better. Remove everything and add the following:

```
body {
  font-family: "Verdana"; margin: 0 auto;
  width: 80%; background-color: #EEEEEE;
}
h1 {
  font-size: 2em; text-decoration: underline;
}
#room-list ul li {
  display: block; cursor: pointer; padding: 10px 10px;
  border: 2px solid #0000FF; border-radius: 10px;
  width: 75%; background-color: #FFFFFF; margin-bottom: 3px;
}
#room-list li.selected {
  background-color: #0000FF; color: #FFFFFF;
}
#room-list input {
  padding: 10px; display: block; width: 90%;
}
#room-list button {
  padding: 10px 20px; margin-top: 20px; background-color: #00FF00;
  text-transform: uppercase; font-weight: bold; cursor: pointer;
}
```

When you are done with these edits, refresh the page and you should see something like this:

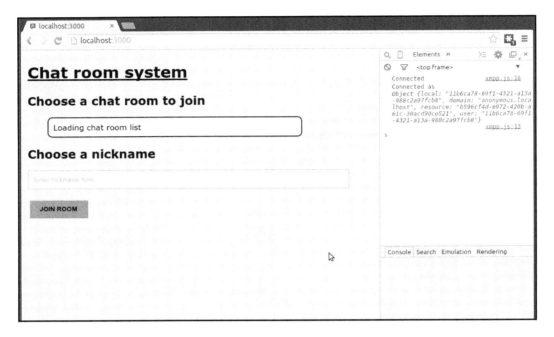

Next we need to update our JavaScript to perform three separate tasks:

1. Load the room list from the server (after login) and write to the screen.
2. Handle the selection of the room and the request to join the room.
3. Handle a failed room join (for example, from a conflicting nickname).

First we'll start with loading the room list. If you remember, we can do this using a `DISCO#items` query on the chat server itself. This will return us a list of chat rooms, so it seems like a good place to start.

Update the `xmpp.connection` event to store the user's JID to the window object. And then let's make another function call to get the room list:

```
socket.on('xmpp.connection', function(data) {
  console.log('Connected as', data.jid)
  window.jid = data.jid
  getRoomList()
})

var getRoomList = function() {
```

```
var request = { of: 'chat.localhost' }
  socket.send('xmpp.discover.items', request, function(error, items) {
    console.log('Received room list', error, items)
    var list = $('#room-list ul')
      /* Remove our placeholder */
      list.find('li').remove()
      items.forEach(function(item) {
        /* Only show the room name */
        var li = $('<li/>')
          .attr('data-jid', item.jid)
          .text(item.name)
          .appendTo(list)
      })
  })
}
```

If you refresh the page now, you should see a list of chat rooms. If not, never fear! It might just be that Prosody has removed them. We can create some chat rooms by opening up Empathy with our test user and adding rooms as we did earlier in the chapter. Once that's done, refresh and try again. Hopefully you now see something along the lines of the following screenshot:

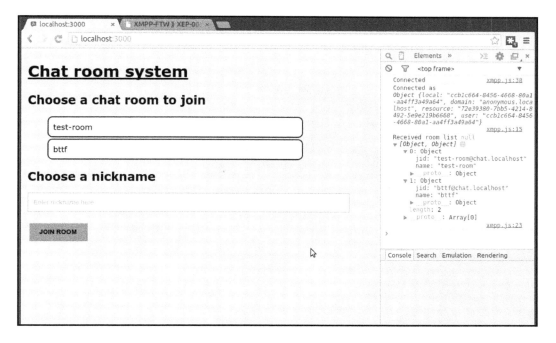

We could take this part of the application further by making an information request to each room in parallel to find out more information such as a name, a description, how many members are currently in the room, and a whole set of information about its configuration. It would certainly be fun but there are only so many pages we can put in this book!

The middle part isn't really XMPP-related, but we need to handle the room selection and nickname validation before attempting to join the room. So, we need to do a few things: first, when the user clicks on a room, add a selected CSS class to the <li/> element (and clear them from any other items in the list); second, store the selected room name; and third, on clicking the button, we need to check that the user has entered a nickname and selected a room (otherwise, we'll add a popup error message).

First to the <li/> element click:

```
$(document).on('click', '#room-list li', function(e) {
    /* Clear any existing selected rooms */
    $('#room-list li.selected').attr('class', '')
    /* Add'selected'CSS class to our new room */
    $(e.target).attr('class', 'selected')
    console.log('Chosen room is now', $(e.target).attr('data-jid'))
})
```

Next, we'll listen for a click on the <button/> and validate that the user has provided the required information:

```
$('#room-list button').click(function() {
  var chosenRoom = $('#room-list li.selected')
  var nickname = $('#room-list input').val()
  if (0 === chosenRoom.length) {
      return alert('You must select a room')
  }
  if (!nickname) {
      return alert('You must enter a nickname')
  }
  var roomJid = chosenRoom.attr('data-jid')
    joinChatRoom(roomJid) /* not written yet! */
})
```

Cool! Now we're ready for the final step of attempting to join the room itself. For this, we use the XMPP-FTW event of xmpp.muc.join. We'll assume that if we start receiving presences (which are sent as xmpp.muc.roster events), then we've joined the room successfully; if not, we'll show the error message to the user. In our example, we'll simulate a nickname conflict.

Picking up from our preceding function, let's make a call to join the room and start things up:

```
var joinChatRoom = function(roomJid, nickname) {
  var request = { room: roomJid, nick: nickname }
  window.mucDetails = request
  socket.send('xmpp.muc.join', request)
}
socket.on('xmpp.muc.error', function(e) {
  console.error('Chat room error', e)
  if (e.error.condition === 'conflict') {
    return alert('Nickname already in use')
  }
  alert('Chat room error: ' + e.error.condition)
})
socket.on('xmpp.muc.roster', function(user) {
  showChatWindow() /* not written yet */
  addUser(user) /* not written yet */
})
```

Now let's simulate our nickname conflict. Errors in XMPP follow a standard format that is described in RFC-6120, but for those more familiar with HTTP error codes, you may find XEP-0086 (http://xmpp.org/extensions/xep-0086.html) useful to review. This also shows the format of XMPP errors. In the case of a nickname conflict, we'll receive an error with a <condition/> child element with a value of conflict. In our preceding function, we look for this and report back to the user of this issue.

Let's log into a chat room with our test user from Empathy, and then attempt to join the same room using our new web-based UI:

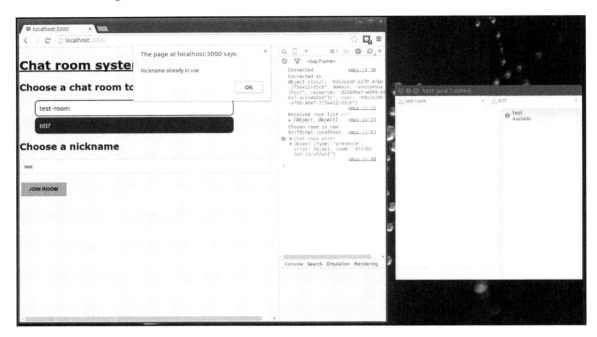

Here on the right, we see our test user in Empathy who has created two rooms, bttf and test-room, both joined with the nickname test. On the left, we can see both of these chat rooms listed in our browser. We've attempted to join the bttf(@chat.localhost room with a nickname of test, which has resulted in our conflict error. Awesome stuff!

Now that we've got our room joining code in place, it's time to head into creating the chat window itself, listing users, messages, and sending messages, too. I hope you're having lots of fun so far!

# Where the action happens

OK, now we're logged in and we have joined a chat room with a nickname. We now need to display our chat interface and get the conversation going. Pop open your HTML file and let's add some chat elements, specifically:

- An area to display a list of users
- A small form to post new messages
- An area to hold the chat messages:

```
<section id="chat-window">
  <h2><em>room@jid</em></h2>
  <div class="chat">
    <dl></dl>
  </div>
  <div class="user-list">
    <ul>
      <li data-role="placeholder">Users will appear here
      </li>
    </ul>
  </div>
  <div class="post">
    <textarea rows="3"></textarea>
    <button type="button">Post</button>
  </div>
</section>
```

We've added some example content to help with styling the UI, so we'll also need to add some CSS. Pop open the style file and add the following:

```
#chat-window {
  display: none; width: 90%; margin: 0 auto;
  height: 100%; position: absolute;
}
#chat-window button {
  padding: 10px 20px; text-transform: uppercase;
  font-weight: bold; float: right; cursor: pointer;
}
#chat-window .chat {
  position: absolute; top: 50px; left: 0px; right: 35%;
  bottom: 75px; overflow: auto; padding: 5px;
  background-color: #FFFFFF;
}
#chat-window .chat dt {
  float: left; width: 80px; overflow: hidden;
}
```

```
#chat-window .chat dt:after {
  content: ': ';
}
#chat-window .chat dd {
  margin-left: 85px;
}
#chat-window .post {
  bottom: 5px; left: 0px; position: absolute; width: 99%;
}
#chat-window .post textarea {
  width: 85%;
}
#chat-window .user-list {
  right: 10px; width: 30%; top: 0px;
  bottom: 75px; position: absolute; overflow: auto;
}
#chat-window .user-list ul {
  padding: 0;
}
#chat-window .user-list ul li {
  display: block; padding: 10px 5px;
  background-color: #FFFFFF; margin-bottom: 3px;
}
```

That should give us enough HTML and CSS to get things going. Now we can start implementing our JavaScript, where there are a few things we need to achieve:

- Display the chat room HTML
- Handle incoming room member details
    1. Current members
    2. New members
    3. Members leaving
- Handle incoming messages
- Allow the user to send messages

We'll make these features work over the next three subsections, and once we're done, we'll have a fully functional (albeit basic) anonymous multi-user chat system!

# Displaying the chat room HTML and handling users

We've already included two unimplemented functions in our code to handle displaying the chat room and handle incoming changes to the users in the room, namely `showChatWindow` and `addUser`. Now let's implement these functions. The first (`showChatWindow`) should be easy; we need to detect weather the chat window is being shown, and if not we hide the room selection page and show our chat window. Let's jump into that:

```
var showChatWindow = function() {
  var isDisplayed = $('#chat-window').is(':visible')
  if (isDisplayed) return; /* Chat window is visible */
  $('#room-list').style('display', 'none')
  $('#chat-window').style('display', 'block')
}
```

All we're doing here is detecting whether the chat room HTML is visible. If not, we make it visible and hide the room selection HTML. Great stuff! Onto the next step, handling users!

The next function we need to implement is `addUser`. If we log out the typical data we receive when we initially join the room, we will see something like the following:

```
{ room: "bttf@chat.localhost", nick: "test", affiliation: "owner", role:
"moderator"}
{ room: "bttf@chat.localhost", nick: "Biff", affiliation: "none", role:
"participant", jid: { domain: "anonymous.localhost", resource:
"8b7a0dd3-316b-40fa-a90b-230497786789", user: "ef3607f8-db8a-4269-9f5c-
a9c41b76e2b2"}, status: [ 110 ] }
```

The first call to `addUser` is from the room owner (connected via our desktop XMPP client). We're told this user has an affiliation of owner and the role of moderator.

The second call tells us about our user. Since we have permission to see our own JID, this is returned to us, and we can see that we've joined the room as someone with the ability to post to the chat room but have no long term affiliation. Additionally, we've received the status element with an entry of value 110, which, as you may remember from before, confirms that this status update is about our user.

Provided with this information, we can now start building the user list by implementing the `addUser` function. In this function, we'll handle three scenarios:

- A nickname that we haven't seen before joins the room
- A nickname we already have has a change of role to none, indicating that they've left the room
- A nickname we already have has their role changed, and so we need to ensure that we don't add them twice

In addition, we'll also need to remove the user list placeholder that appears when the chat window is first loaded. As the nickname is unique, we'll be able to use this to track the users in the DOM:

```
var addUser = function(user) {
  /* remove the placeholder */
  $('li[data-role="placeholder"]').remove()
  var userEntry = $('.user-list li[data-nick="' + user.nick + '"]')
  if (0 === userEntry.length) return newUser(user)
  if ('none' === user.role) return removeUser(userEntry)
  /* Otherwise we have nothing to do */
}
var newUser = function(user) {
  cssClass = ''
  if (user.status && (-1 !== user.status.indexOf(110))) {
    cssClass = 'current-user'
  }
  entry = '<li data-nick="' + user.nick
    + '" class="' + cssClass + '">'
    + user.nick + '</li>'
  $('.user-list ul').append(entry)
}
var removeUser = function(user) {
  user.remove()
}
```

As we added a CSS class of `current-user` to our own entry in the room user list, let's add some CSS to show us who we are:

```
#chat-window .user-list ulli.current-user:after {
  content: ' (you)';
}
```

Great! Now if we reload the page and join a room, we should see a user list in place, including an entry highlighting who we are!

# Handling incoming messages

Next, we're going to handle incoming messages (since there's no point sending a message if we can't see responses, right?). Incoming messages using XMPP-FTW arrive via the xmpp.muc.message event. Here's a typical payload:

```
{
  content: "Hello Biff!",
  nick: "test",
  private: false,
  room: "bttf@chat.localhost"
}
```

The payload tells us which room the message came from, the nickname of the sender, whether it was a private message or not, and the content of the message. Given that our anonymous user will be logged into only a single room at a time, we can ignore the room key and just handle writing the nickname and content to the screen. At the same time, we can flag that the message is from our user and whether it's a private message or not. We won't be coding up sending private messages here (feel free to extend the project though!).

Our chat messages will be held in the definition list using the <dt/> (nickname) and <dd/> (content) tags. We already have the CSS in place to handle the positioning. The only other thing we'll need to do is ensure that when we add a message, the chat area itself is scrolled to the bottom.

So, to handle our messages, let's put together the following code:

```
var addMessage = function(message) {
  if (!message.content) return /* ignore non-content messages */
  var cssClass = ''
  if (message.private) cssClass += 'muc-private'
  if (message.nick === window.mucDetails.nick) {
    cssClass += 'muc-current-user'
  }
  var dt = $('<dt class="' + cssClass + '"/>')
  dt.text(message.nick)
  var dd = $('<dd class="' + cssClass + '"/>')
  dd.text(message.content)
    /* If the message mentions us, highlight it */
  var regex = new RegExp(window.mucDetails.nick, 'gi')
  var replace = '<strong>' + window.mucDetails.nick + '</strong>'
```

```
    dd.html(dd.html().replace(regex, replace))
    $('.chat dl').append(dt)
    $('.chat dl').append(dd)
    /* Scroll to bottom of chat area */
    $('.chat').scrollTop($('.chat')[0].scrollHeight)
  }
  socket.on('xmpp.muc.message', addMessage)
```

We'll also need some CSS to highlight private messages and messages posted by the users themselves:

```
#chat-window .muc-private { color: red; }
#chat-window .muc-current-user { color: blue; }
```

# Sending a message

I hope that at this point, you've realized we've got something cool going on and that it's now time to start sending messages back! To send messages, we use the reverse event, `xmpp.muc.message`. The MUC room will relay the message back to us, so it will reuse our `addMessage` function from before to display our outgoing message:

```
$('#chat-window button').click(function() {
  var chatMsg = $('.post textarea')
  if (!chatMsg.val()) return
  var message = {
    room: window.mucDetails.room,
    content: chatMsg.val()
  }
  socket.send('xmpp.muc.message', message)
  chatMsg.val('')
})
```

In the preceding code, we listen for clicks on the `Post` button. Then, if we have content to send, we fire off an event before setting the `textarea` to empty so that it is ready for our next message to go out.

# Wrapping up

In a short amount of time, we've learned the basics of multi-user chat in XMPP. Furthermore, we've built a simple anonymous chat room system in fewer than 200 lines of code! In addition, because the chat room is written using XMPP, other users can join from their own clients and even from their own remote servers (to which they have clients connected directly), without any additional code or effort! Pretty cool stuff.

The project we've built is basic and there's a lot more you can add to it with little effort or additional code. If you think about it, we've built the basics of what could be a chat system for a website with multiple topics, or even with a little bit of work a customer service system for employees at a company.

While basic and not hugely robust, the code is available for you to experiment with in the book's source repository. Have fun!

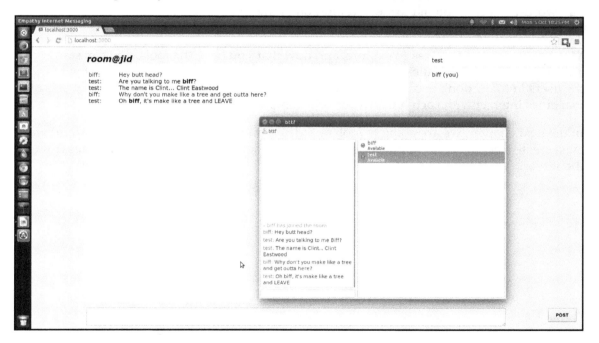

# Summary

In this chapter, we learned about the vary basics of multi-user chat in XMPP. That said, we still went on to build a couple of really exciting small projects, which can be the stepping stones to much more powerful and useful applications, both for server tasks and to increase interaction on websites.

There's still a large amount we haven't covered with MUCs, but as always, they are openly documented on the XMPP website, and specifically in XEP-0045 (`http://xmpp.org/extens ions/xep-45.html`).

There are several things that we did not cover in this chapter. These include invites, message history, reserved nicknames, banning users, leaving a room, converting a one-to-one chat to a multi-user chat, requesting the ability to post messages in a chat room (if you don't have the ability by default), approving/denying those requests, and joining a password-protected room. Further exploration of the XEPs will reveal the details of how these capabilities can be developed.

Multi-user chat is a fun area to explore, and now that you have the tools, you can start building up your ideas quickly and easily whil leaning on the power of XMPP. Don't forget, the users in MUC don't necessarily have to be a person. They can be used such that sets of machines interact with each other to perform complex tasks!

In the next chapter, we are going to look at XMPP's publish/subscribe mechanism, and we'll even create a client/server application in which the client receives real-time updates from the server!

# 6
# Make Your Static Website Real-Time

OK, now we're really starting to get moving with XMPP and we still haven't even begun to scratch the surface. In this chapter, we're going to start increasing our speed towards 88 mph! Maybe not quite, but we are going to introduce a very important area of XMPP (something from which many, many other protocols and projects are built), and that's Publish-Subscribe, or `pubsub` for short. The original pubsub specification was documented in XEP-0060 (`http://www.xmpp.org/extensions/xep-0060.html`) and, while having some extensions, has remained fairly solid. So once we've covered some basics, we're just going to dive right into some practical work and learn how to make our static website real-time with very little code or effort using XMPP.

Pubsub is used extensively by many different companies in many different sectors. For example, it is often used to build real-time monitoring systems, social networks, and Internet of Things (IoT) setups, often with a small bit of business logic on top of the base pubsub specification (but keeping interactions with clients the same).

## Are we there yet?

Pubsub at its core is really a simple concept. There is a store of data to which you subscribe; you can retrieve information from this data store, and when there are updates, you are told about them. While it is a simple concept, it is also a very powerful one because it's hard to think of an application that doesn't use some form of publish/subscribe arrangement, a database for example.

One of the advantages is that once the server receives this stream opener and knows that it is configured for a component on this address it responds to XMPP. Pubsub is that clients that do not need to poll the server for updates (or the "are we there yet?" syndrome) but will get pushed updates when they happen. This property of pubsub makes it ideal for building real-time systems as it reduces the load on the server from polling and ensures that data is received by clients as soon as possible.

# Interacting with Publish-Subscribe

Let's imagine we're sitting with Marty McFly in the DeLorean waiting for the exact time to put his foot on the accelerator and head back to the future. To get this information, he has been told by Doc Brown to use an XMPP pubsub system because Doc knows it's real-time and reliable.

First, Marty would need to find the XMPP server, discover where he can get information from it, subscribe to the source of the information, get some history, and then start receiving real-time updates. Meanwhile, Doc would need to have these pieces of information created and published to the server.

# Discovery

As with all other parts of XMPP, if we want to discover and find information about a pubsub provider, we use our old friend (by now, right?) DISCO. Pubsub systems will often sit on their own domain under an XMPP server domain (often running as a component; more on that in the next chapter).

To discover a pubsub system, Marty would run a DISCO#items query against the parent domain and see what was available:

```
<iq type='get' id='query1'
from='marty@mcfly.fam/street'
to='hill.valley'>
  <query xmlns='http://jabber.org/protocol/disco#items'/>
</iq>
```

The server then responds with a set of items that it's hosting:

```
<iq type='result' id='query1'
from='hill.valley'
to='marty@mcfly.fam/street'>
  <query xmlns='http://jabber.org/protocol/disco#items>
    <item jid='pubsub.hill.valley'/>
    <item jid='chat.hill.valley'/>
    <item jid='identity.hill.valley'/>
  </query>
</iq>
```

When Marty looks at this response, he thinks that the pubsub.hill.valleysub-domain may be interesting, so he runs a DISCO#info query against it to find out more:

```
<iq type='get' id='query2'
from='marty@mcfly.fam/street'
to='pubsub.hill.valley'>
  <query xmlns='http://jabber.org/protocol/disco#info'/>
</iq>
```

The server now responds, telling him more about itself and what features it supports:

```
<iq type='result' id='query2'
from='hill.valley'
to='marty@mcfly.fam/street'>
  <query xmlns='http://jabber.org/protocol/disco#info'>
    <identity
category='pubsub'
name='Hill Valley PubSub'
type='service'/>
      <feature var='http://jabber.org/protocol/pubsub'/>
  </query>
</iq>
```

As a user, we think this may be interesting. It is certainly a pubsub server, so we do a bit more digging to see what endpoints are available:

```
<iq type='get' id='query3
from='marty@mcfly.fam/street'
to='pubsub.hill.valley'>
  <query xmlns='http://jabber.org/protocol/disco#items'/>
</iq>
```

With the server duly replying with the following:

```
<iq type='result' id='query3'
from='pubsub.hill.valley'
to='marty@mcfly.fam/street'>
  <query xmlns='http://jabber.org/protocol/disco#items>
    <item jid='pubsub.hill.valley'
node='storm-updates'
description='Hill Valley storm updates'/>
    <item jid='pubsub.hill.valley'
node='doc-brown-weather-experiment'/>
  </query>
</iq>
```

Now if you're Marty sitting in the DeLorean, waiting for the incoming storm and forDoc to prepare the clock tower, these two `pubsub` nodes would be very useful, right?

What is a node?
A node is simply an identifier for a location of a data store. You could compare it with a database table, a handle on Twitter, or a friend's feed on Facebook.

The next thing he might want to do is find out a little more about each of these nodes. Marty could run `DISCO#info` queries on them to find out more. Let's start with the storm updates node:

```
<iq type='get' id='query4'
from='marty@mcfly.fam/street'
to='pubsub.hill.valley'>
  <query xmlns='http://jabber.org/protocol/disco#info'
   node='storm-updates'/>
</iq>
```

The server then responds with information about this node:

```
<iq type='result' id='query4'
from='hill.valley'
to='marty@mcfly.fam/street'>
  <query xmlns='http://jabber.org/protocol/disco#info>
    <identity category='pubsub' type='leaf'/>
    <feature var='http://jabber.org/protocol/pubsub'/>
    <x xmlns='jabber:x:data' type='result'>
      <field var='FORM_TYPE' type='hidden'>
        <value>http://jabber.org/protocol/pubsub#meta-data</value>
      </field>
      <field var='pubsub#type' label='Payload type'
       type='textsingle'>
```

```
            <value>http://www.w3.org/2005/Atom</value>
        </field>
        <field var='pubsub#title' label='Title' type='text-single'>
            <value>Storm updates</value>
        </field>
        <field var='pubsub#description' label='Description'
         type='text-single'>
            <value>Real-time and historical updates on Hill Valley
                storms </value>
        </field>
    </x>
  </query>
</iq>
```

Here, the node identifies itself as a pubsub node but then goes on to provide us with a whole bunch of additional information in the format of a data form (it's nice how we keep seeing these standard patterns appear, right?). The data form identifies the kind of data that is held within it, using the FORM_TYPE field. From there, it goes on to describe the properties of the node, such as the data format used (in this case, **ATOM**), and gives the node a title and description. Great stuff! Marty should subscribe to this later and get updates on the storm's progress.

Next, he attempts to find more information about the curious node that Doc Brown has created for his Weather Experiment:

```
<iq type='get' id='query5'
from='marty@mcfly.fam/street'
to='pubsub.hill.valley'>
  <query xmlns='http://jabber.org/protocol/disco#info'
    node='doc-brown-weather-experiment'/>
</iq>
```

He receive the following:

```
<iq type='result' id='query5'
from='hill.valley'
to='marty@mcfly.fam/street'>
  <query xmlns='http://jabber.org/protocol/disco#info>
    <identity category='pubsub' type='leaf'/>
    <feature var='http://jabber.org/protocol/pubsub'/>
    <x xmlns='jabber:x:data' type='result'>
      <field var='FORM_TYPE' type='hidden'>
        <value>http://jabber.org/protocol/pubsub#meta-data</value>
      </field>
      <field var='pubsub#title' label='Title' type='text-single'>
        <value>Doc's weather experiment</value>
      </field>
```

```
        <field var='pubsub#creator' label='Creator' type='jid-single'>
          <value>doc@brown.sci</value>
        </field>
      </x>
    </query>
  </iq>
```

It seems as though Doc either created his node in a hurry or didn't want to give too much information away about his node. Maybe, we'll be able to find out more soon!

# Subscribing

Now that Marty has discovered these two useful nodes, he will need to subscribe to them. This is done rather simply, using the following stanzas:

```
<iq type='set' id='sub1'
from='marty@mcfly.fam/street'
to='pubsub.hill.valley'>
  <pubsub xmlns='http://jabber.org/protocol/pubsub'>
    <subscribe node='storm-updates' jid='marty@mcfly.fam'/>
  </pubsub>
</iq>
<iq type='set' id='sub2'
    from='marty@mcfly.fam/street'
    to='pubsub.hill.valley'>
  <pubsub xmlns='http://jabber.org/protocol/pubsub'>
    <subscribe node='doc-brown-weather-experiment'
      jid='marty@mcfly.fam'/>
  </pubsub>
</iq>
```

The subscription requests come back almost immediately:

```
<iq type='result' id='sub1'
from='pubsub.hill.valley'
to='marty@mcfly.fam/street'>
  <pubsub xmlns='http://jabber.org/protocol/pubsub>
    <subscription node='storm-updates'jid='marty@mcfly.fam'
      subscription='subscribed'/>
  </pubsub>
</iq>
<iq type='result' id='sub2'
from='pubsub.hill.valley'
to='marty@mcfly.fam/street'>
  <pubsub xmlns='http://jabber.org/protocol/pubsub>
    <subscription node='doc-brown-weather-experiment' jid='marty@mcfly.fam'
```

```
            subscription='pending'/>
      </pubsub>
   </iq>
```

Marty is now subscribed to the storm-updates node, as we can see from the subscription attribute value in the subscription element. But curiously, his subscription for **doc-brown-weather-experiment** is pending. What could that mean?

# Subscriptions, affiliations, and access models

When users create `pubsub` nodes (or update their configuration later), they have the ability to set permissions for the node. These permissions allow them to control who can subscribe to a node, and once they are subscribed, what their affiliation will be, for example, read-only, publish, and so on.

The `pubsub` specification defines a set of access models by default, ranging from most restricted to least restricted:

- **Whitelist**: Only a specific set of JIDs will be allowed to successfully subscribe to the node
- **Authorize**: When a subscription request is made, the owner must manually approve it
- **Roster**: If the user is contained within a specific roster group, then they will be allowed to subscribe
- **Presence**: Only JIDs with an allowed presence subscription may be allowed to subscribe to the node
- **Open**: Anyone can subscribe to the node and will be automatically approved

So it would seem that the storm-updates node was created with an open access model (since we became automatically subscribed). However, Doc must have created the Doc-brown-weather-experiment node with an authorize access model to prevent people from reading his updates. This must mean that he's posting updates about his progress in setting things up for the time machine! Hopefully, he'll authorize Marty's subscription request soon!

When it comes to subscriptions, there are an additional couple of levels outside of `subscribed` and `pending`. The other, as you can probably guess is `none`, meaning the user has no subscription at all. The last is `unconfigured`, which means that the user has a subscription, but they need to configure their options, such as whether they'd like to receive the body of any new items with a push notification or not. Full details on node subscription configurations can be found in XEP-0060.

In addition to having a subscription to a node, a user will also have an **affiliation**. An affiliation describes which features of the node they are able to access, such as retrieving posts or publishing new posts themselves.

The affiliation types are defined as follows:

- **Owner**: The owner has the ability to control every aspect of the node
- **Publisher**: The ability to publish to the node, retrieve items, and delete existing items
- **Publish-Only**: The ability to publish to the node, but not to subscribe or retrieve any items from it
- **Member**: The ability to subscribe to and retrieve items from the node, but not to publish
- **None**: Essentially, the user has no link with the node at the present time
- **Outcast**: Banned from any interactions with the node

 It's quite possible to have multiple subscriptions to a node, but set up with different subscription options by defining either an options subscription ID or by subscribing using a full JID rather than a bare one. This means that on a desktop, push notifications could include the full content of new items, whereas on a mobile, we would only receive the notification itself. So the device can decide to go off and get the full item based on its current connection or battery status, for example.

Meanwhile, back at the clock tower, Doc Brown receives a push notification on his XMPP client:

```
<message id='notify1'
from='pubsub.hill.valley'
to='doc@brown.sci/experiment'>
  <x xmlns='jabber:x:data' type='form'>
    <title>PubSub subscriber request</title>
    <field var='FORM_TYPE' type='hidden'>
      <value>
        http://jabber.org/protocol/pubsub#subscribe_authorization
      </value>
```

```
    </field>
    <field var='pubsub#node' type='text-single' label='Node ID'>
      <value>doc-brown-weather-experiment</value>
    </field>
    <field var='pusub#subscriber_jid' type='jid-single'
     label='Subscriber Address'>
      <value>marty@mcfly.fam</value>
    </field>
    <field var='pubsub#allow' type='boolean'
          label='Allow this JID to subscribe to this pubsub node?'>
      <value>false</value>
    </field>
  </x>
</iq>
```

It's a subscription request for his weather experiment node from none other than Marty. As Doc wants Marty to receive his updates, he immediately fires back an approval:

```
<message id='approve1'
from='doc@brown.sci/experiment'
to='pubsub.hill.valley'>
  <x xmlns='jabber:x:data' type='submit'>
    <field var='FORM_TYPE' type='hidden'>
      <value>
        http://jabber.org/protocol/pubsub#subscribe_authorization
      </value>
    </field>
    <field var='pubsub#node'>
      <value>doc-brown-weather-experiment</value>
    </field>
    <field var='pubsub#subscriber_jid'>
      <value>marty@mcfly.fam</value>
    </field>
    <field var='pubsub#allow'>
      <value>true</value>
    </field>
  </x>
</iq>
```

Once this approval is received by the pubsub server, a notification is pushed back to Marty to immediately let him know that his subscription status has changed:

```
<message id='notify1'
from='pubsub.hill.valley'
to='doc@brown.sci/experiment'>
  <event xmlns='http://jabber.org/protocol/pubsub#event'>
    <subscription node='doc-brown-weather-experiment'
          jid='marty@mcfly.fam' subscription='subscribed'/>
  </event>
</message>
```

Now Marty is subscribed to Doc Brown's weather experiment node. He'll be able to request historical items and receive push notifications for new posts.

 As a node owner, it's possible to retrieve a list of subscriptions and affiliations to a node as well as modify subscriptions and affiliations separately. Additionally, a user can request a list of their subscriptions and affiliations and the nodes to which they reply from a server with a simple IQ request.

# Creating and configuring nodes

One thing that you may have been wondering throughout the last section is; how Doc Brown created and configured his node in the first place? Well it's your lucky day because that's exactly what we are going to find out now!

Creating and configuring a node can be done in one of two ways: either we create and configure at the same time, or we first create our node and then configure it later. We'll show the create-then-configure setup here, but you can find details of the single-step approach in XEP-0060.

Creating a node is a rather simple affair. Doc Brown would probably have sent an IQ stanza that looked just like this:

```
<iq type='set' id='create1'
from='doc@brown.sci/experiment'
to='pubsub.hill.valley'>
  <pubsub xmlns='http://jabber.org/protocol/pubsub'>
    <create node='doc-brown-weather-experiment'/>
  </pubsub>
</iq>
```

The server would then determine whether the user was able to create that node. It could send an error for reasons such as the node already existing or the user not having permission to create nodes. Obviously, Doc Brown was able to create his node, so he would have received a simple result type IQ stanza:

```
<iq type='result' id='create1'
from='pubsub.hill.valley'
to='doc@brown.sci/experiment'>
  <pubsub xmlns='http://jabber.org/protocol/pubsub'>
    <create node='doc-brown-weather-experiment'/>
  </pubsub>
</iq>
```

The next thing Doc would have wanted to do is configure the node so that only those users who he allowed would be able to subscribe and read his posts (and receive the push updates).What Doc would do is first request a configuration form from the server to determine all the configuration options available:

```
<iq type='get' id='config1'
from='doc@brown.sci/experiment'
to='pubsub.hill.valley'>
  <pubsub xmlns='http://jabber.org/protocol/pubsub'>
    <configure node='doc-brown-weather-experiment'/>
  </pubsub>
</iq>
```

The server would respond with a list of configuration options (and their default/current value if set); here's a truncated listing:

```
<iq type='result' id='config1'
from='pubsub.hill.valley'
to='doc@brown.sci/experiment'>
  <pubsub xmlns='http://jabber.org/protocol/pubsub'>
    <configure node='doc-brown-weather-experiment'>
      <x xmlns='jabber:x:data' type='form'>
        <field var='FORM_TYPE' type='hidden'>
          <value>
            http://jabber.org/protocol/pubsub#node_config
          </value>
        </field>
        <field var='pubsub#title' type='text-single'
               label='Title'/>
        <field var='pubsub#deliver_notifications' type='boolean'
               label='Whether to deliver event notifications'>
          <value>true</value>
        </field>
        <field var='pubsub#access_model' type='list-single'
```

```
                  label='Specify the subscriber model'>
          <option><value>authorize</value></option>
          <option><value>open</value></option>
          <option><value>presence</value></option>
          <option><value>roster</value></option>
          <option><value>whitelist</value></option>
          <value>open</value>
        </field>
      </x>
    </configure>
  </pubsub>
</iq>
```

As we can see, by default the server created Doc's node with an open access model, which he'd quickly want to change to authorize model to an prevent anyone from subscribing without his knowledge (of course, he can always change their subscription later):

```
<iq type='set' id='config2'
from='doc@brown.sci/experiment'
to='pubsub.hill.valley'>
  <pubsub xmlns='http://jabber.org/protocol/pubsub'>
    <configure node='doc-brown-weather-experiment'>
      <x xmlns='jabber:x:data' type='submit'>
        <field var='FORM_TYPE' type='hidden'>
          <value>
            http://jabber.org/protocol/pubsub#node_config
          </value>
        </field>
        <field var='pubsub#title'>
          <value>Doc's weather experiment</value>
        </field>
        <field var='pubsub#deliver_notifications'>
          <value>true</value>
        </field>
        <field var='pubsub#access_model'>
          <value>authorize</value>
        </field>
      </x>
    </configure>
  </pubsub>
</iq>
```

To this, the server would respond with a simple result IQ stanza. Should the node have subscribers, and should the node be configured to do so, the server could also push the updated configuration to each member of the node, informing them of the new settings.

# Retrieving items

Back to Marty anxiously sitting in the DeLorean time machine. He has just been pushed a notification saying that he now has a subscription to Doc Brown's weather experiment node, so he'd probably like to get the last few items from that node and see what Doc has been up to.

To retrieve the last few items from the node, Marty makes a request:

```
<iq type='get' id='retrieve1'
from='marty@mcfly.fam/street'
to='pubsub.hill.valley'>
  <pubsub xmlns='http://jabber.org/protocol/pubsub'>
    <items node='doc-brown-weather-experiment'/>
    <set xmlns='http://jabber.org/protocol/rsm'>
      <max>3</max>
      <before/>
    </set>
  </pubsub>
</iq>
```

In this request, we're asking for items from the Doc-brown-weather-experiment node. You'll also notice a new element with an unfamiliar namespace that represents **Result Set Management** or **RSM**.

Result set management is another one of those wonderful standard patterns in XMPP that pops up all over the place, and is defined in XEP-0059 (http://xmpp.org/extensions/xep -59.html). For requests, it allows a user to request a restricted number of items (<max/>) and to page through items using an identifier (which depends on the data they are requesting) using a set of additional child elements, for example, <before/>, <after/>, and <index/>.

In the preceding example, Marty asks for at most three items from Doc's weather experiment node (as indicated by the <max/> tag), and asks the server page lists the items from most recent to least recent items (as indicated by the <before/> tag). If the oldest item came back with an ID of post-id-10, for example, and he wanted to request the next set of previous results, he could modify his query to read the ID and the server would return the paged results as expected:

```
<iq type='get' id='retrieve1'
from='marty@mcfly.fam/street'
to='pubsub.hill.valley'>
  <pubsub xmlns='http://jabber.org/protocol/pubsub'>
    <items node='doc-brown-weather-experiment'/>
    <set xmlns='http://jabber.org/protocol/rsm'>
```

```
        <max>3</max>
        <before>post-id-10</before>
      </set>
    </pubsub>
  </iq>
```

When the items come back from Marty's request, the request will probably contain an equivalent RSM element describing the total number of items, ignoring the query and the IDs of the first and last items to help with pagination of results.

Anyway, Marty's request would probably come back looking something like the following:

```
<iq type='result' id='retrieve1'
from='pubsub.hill.valley'
to='marty@mcfly.fam/street'>
  <pubsub xmlns='http://jabber.org/protocol/pubsub'>
    <items node='doc-brown-weather-experiment'>
      <item id='expt-post-5'>
        <body>Recovered from my slip</body>
      </item>
      <item id='expt-post-6'>
        <body>A tree has fallen on the wire :(</body>
      </item>
      <item id='expt-post-7'>
        <body>I'll zip slide down!</body>
      </item>
    </items>
    <set xmlns='http://jabber.org/protocol/rsm'>
      <first index='5'>expt-post-5</first>
      <last>expt-post-7</first>
      <count>7</count>
    </set>
  </pubsub>
</iq>
```

In this response, we get three items with Doc's latest updates. The RSM element tells us that, within the returned results, the first item had an ID of `expt-post-5` and the last had `expt-post-7`, with there being a total of seven updates from Doc during the evening.

Before requesting items, we could have made a `DISCO#items` query against the node first. This would have returned a list of all the items in the node by ID (probably with an RSM element if there were too many results for one response stanza), which means that we could potentially have cherry-picked posts by ID or just received an idea of how many total posts were in the node (requested with `<max/>` set to items and looking at the `<count/>` element in the response). Marty is now up to date with Doc's progress. Now he has to await any updates…

# Publishing items

Back at the clock tower, Doc is flying down the zip line at breakneck speed. Upon reaching the street, he reconnects the wire from the clock to the cable suspended across the street. It's time to update his `pubsub` node and let Marty know. He retrieves his XMPP device and starts furiously typing away to create the following stanza:

```
<iq type='set' id='publish1'
from='doc@brown.sci/experiment'
to='pubsub.hill.valley'>
  <pubsub xmlns='http://jabber.org/protocol/pubsub'>
    <publish node='doc-brown-weather-experiment'>
      <item>
        <body>Wire reconnected, we're good to go!</body>
      </item>
    </publish>
  </publish>
</iq>
```

We can, if we want, post an item with a specific ID by adding an attribute to the `<item/>` element. This makes `pubsub` nodes great places to store key-value data for retrieval by users, for use in applications for example.

The `pubsub` server receives Doc's request and reports back to him the as well as the ID number that it has generated for his new post:

```
<iq type='result' id='publish1'
from='pubsub.hill.valley'
to='doc@brown.sci/experiment'>
  <pubsub xmlns='http://jabber.org/protocol/pubsub'>
    <publish node='doc-brown-weather-experiment'>
      <item id='expt-post-8'/>
    </publish>
  </pubsub>
</iq>
```

With that, Doc knows that his post has made it successfully to the server, and Marty will receive an update immediately. Speaking of which, Marty's XMPP device suddenly makes a beeping noise and the following stanza appears on his screen:

```
<message from='pubsub.hill.valley'
to='marty@mcfly.fam/street' id='published1'>
  <event xmlns='http://jabber.org/protocol/pubsub#event'>
    <items node='doc-brown-weather-experiment'>
      <item id='expt-post-8'>
        <body>Wire reconnected, we're good to go!</body>
      </item>
```

```
    </items>
  </event>
</message>
```

Marty breathes a sigh of relief as he moves one step closer to going back to the future!

 Depending on the node/server configuration, the user may need to send a directed presence request to the server, informing it that they are online and would like to receive push notifications. Other servers will send them regardless and use the user's server to push the delayed message to them the next time they are online.

# Making your website real-time

In this section, we're going to look at making a static website real-time. To do this, we'll build both a server-side (publishing) and a client-side (subscribing) system. The server-side publisher will write some fake stock market data to a node (because stock values are the bread and butter of real-time system examples, right?). On the client-side, we'll subscribe, pull some historic data from the node, and then await real-time updates writing them to the screen. By the end of the code, you'll be able to build a really quick, simple, and real-time website to bring the cool to your website.

## Configuring Prosody

Once again, we'll need to delve into the Prosody configuration file to set up a `pubsub` service on our XMPP server. Thankfully, the Prosody team has built a basic `pubsub` system that we can use in our development (we'll want a full implementation in a production deployment, though).

Fire up your terminal and let's edit the Prosody configuration file (remember on, Ubuntu, this is in `/etc/prosody/prosody.cfg.lua`). At the bottom of the file, we'll add the following lines:

```
Component "pubsub.localhost" "pubsub"  autocreate_on_publish = true;
    admins = { "bot@localhost" };
```

Once you've saved the file, restart `prosody` and we'll have a `pubsub` service up and running at `pubsub.localhost`.

The two options we set are to create a node when we first publish to it (saving us some setup) and to add our server-side bot user to the list of admins that can create a node.

# Building a server-side publishing mechanism

As we know, we can publish in whatever format we'd like to publish a `pubsub` node, thanks to XML; an element and a namespace are all that clients need to identify and understand if they can handle the data. This may be mixing things up somewhat, but as we're going to ultimately push data to a browser and as we're working with JavaScript, it makes sense to publish JSON formatted data to our pubsub node.

Let's start as we usually do, by working from a clone of the `xmpp-ftw` skeleton project, and installing `node-xmpp-client`:

```
cd ~
git clone git@github.com:xmpp-ftw/skeleton-project.gitpubsub-example
cd pubsub-example
npm install --save node-xmpp-client
```

Next, let's create and edit a file called `publisher.js`, where we'll create our publishing code:

```
const Client = require('node-xmpp-client')
const client = new Client({
  jid: 'bot@localhost',
  password: 'tellnoone',
  host: 'localhost'
})
client.on('online', () => {
  setInterval(publishStockValue, 250)
})
```

In our `publishStockValue` function, we're now going to start publishing data to our `pubsub` node. First, we'll need to generate some fake stock data:

```
let stockValue = 500
const maximumChange = 10
let change = 0
cost generateStockValue = () => {
  change = parseInt(Math.pow(Math.random(), 2) * maximumChange)
  if (Math.random() < 0.5) change *= -1
  stockValue += change
  if ((change < 0) && (Math.abs(change) >stockValue)) {
    change = -1 * stockValue
    stockValue = 0
  }
}
```

Here we're starting from a stock value of 500, and then generating a new value by either adding or deducting a maximum amount of 10 units whilst protecting ourselves from a negative stock value (weighted towards small changes). We can now use this function in our publishing code. Let's now write our `publishStockValue` method:

```
let id = 10
const publishStockValue = () => {
  generateStockValue()
  const dateString = new Date().toISOString()
  const stanza = new Client.ltx.Element('iq', { to: 'pubsub.localhost,
   type: 'set', id: ++id })
  stanza.c('pubsub', { xmlns: 'http://jabber.org/protocol/pubsub'
 })
  .c('publish', { node: 'stock-data-btc-rules' })
  .c('item', { id: dateString })
  .c('json', { xmlns: 'urn:xmpp:json:0' })
  .t(JSON.stringify({ value: stockValue, change: change, timestamp:
dateString }))
  client.send(stanza)
}
```

Note that we've forced the item to be published with a specified ID. We could just have equally left the item ID out and let the server generate a random ID for us. In that case the preceding code would generate a stanza for us that looks like the following:

```
<iq to="pubsub.localhost" type="set" id="22">
  <pubsub xmlns="http://jabber.org/protocol/pubsub">
    <publish node="stock-data">
      <item id="2015-10-19T21:59:30.343Z">
        <json xmlns="urn:xmpp:json:0">
          {"value":522,"change":6,"timestamp":"2015-10-19T21:59:30.343Z"}
        </json>
      </item>
    </publish>
  </pubsub>
</iq>
```

What we've done here is created a JSON-formatted `pubsub` item and published it to a node called `stock-data-btc-rules` on the pubsub service `pubsub.localhost`. The data we've published includes the date of the update, the current price, and the last change value. Note that we haven't included an ID for the item as we'll let the server generate a unique value for us.

The specification for including JSON data within an XMPP XML data can be found in XEP-0335 at `https://xmpp.org/extensions/xep-0335.html`.

With this small amount of code, we're now publishing data to our fake stock data on the server. Hopefully, you'll quickly be able to see how you can adapt this to other pieces of information, such as server performance data, temperature readings, and much more. If there's information that people would be interested in subscribing to, you can publish it just remember that there may be a standard already in place for that type of data, which would make it much quicker and easier for others to process! You can check for standards through the XEPs. The next step will be to write our simple client.

## Building our real-time client

Now that we're publishing to a node on the server, it's time to start making our website real-time! For this example, we're going to connect to the server (anonymously, as in `Chapter 5`, *Building a Multi-User Chat (MUC) Application*), subscribe to the stock node, and retrieve a page of existing results. Then we'll let the server know that we'd like to start receiving data updates through pubsub.

# Setting up the server

To visualize the stock numbers coming from our `pubsub` node, we're going to use the real-time charting library **Smoothie** (`http://smoothiecharts.org`) and, once again, the `XMPP-FTW` skeleton project. Let's begin:

```
cd ~
git clone git@github.com:xmpp-ftw/skeleton-project.git pubsub-example
cd pubsub-example
```

Before installing all the project dependencies, we're going to change the `package.json` file. Open the file and remove the line under dependencies for `xmpp-ftw-buddycloud` (since we won't' be using that module in this project). Once saved, we can install the `xmpp-ftwpubsub` extension:

```
npm i .
npm i --save xmpp-ftw-pubsub
```

Next, we'll update the server so that it only responds to pubsub-related events (although in production we'd want to lock it down further to specific events only). In `index.js` we're going to clear the default listeners and add our `pubsub` extension. Open the project's `index.js` file and where the connection event listener is, we'll update the code to read:

```
primus.on('connection', (socket) => {
  console.log('Websocket connection made')
  const xmppFtw = new xmpp.Xmpp(socket)
  xmppFtw.clearListeners()
  xmppFtw.addListener(new Pubsub())
  socket.xmppFtw = xmppFtw
})
```

Before we start the code, we have to import the additional module. Near the top of the file, we need to find this line:

```
, Buddycloud = require('xmpp-ftw-buddycloud')
```

We will then replace it with the following:

```
, Pubsub = require('xmpp-ftw-pubsub')
```

# Lining up our static website

The next stage is to put together a simple website with some static content, into which we'll be able to drop our super, amazing, awesome real-time display. If we open our main index page `index.ejs` (in the `views` directory), we can create a static page something like the following:

```
<html>
  <head>
    <meta charset="UTF-8" />
      <link rel="stylesheet" type="text/css" href="/css/style.css">
      <script type="text/javascript" src="/scripts/primus.js"></script>
      <script type="text/javascript"
        src="https://code.jquery.com/jquery-2.1.0.min.js"></script>
      <script type="text/javascript"
        src="https://cdnjs.cloudflare.com/ajax/libs/smoothie/1.27.0
        /smoothie.min.js">
      </script>
      <script type="text/javascript" src="/scripts/xmpp.js"></script>
        <title>Just another boring static site?</title>
  </head>
  <body>
    <div id="container">
```

```
    <h1>Just another boring static site?</h1>
    <p>Its a fact that 99.183% of users find static websites boring
        and wished they have some real-time updates*</p>
    <canvas id="chart" width="600" height="100"></canvas>
    <p>
      <em>* especially when driven by open-standards based federated
        systems.</em>
    </p>
  </div>
 </body>
</html>
```

Of course, you can make the content whatever you like. The two important changes are that we load the Smoothie charting library from `cdnjs` and add a canvas element in the content somewhere.

# Let's get real-time...

OK, now that we have our static site set up, its time to start adding real-time components. As we said at the top of this section, we're going to do four things:

- Connect anonymously to the server
- Subscribe to the pubsub node
- Retrieve a page of historical results
- Tell the server we're online and receive real-time updates

We've already learned about anonymous server connections, so remembering back to Chapter 5, *Building a Multi-User Chat (MUC) Application*, we will edit the `xmpp.js` file to read as follows:

```
$(window.document).ready(function() {
  var socket = new Primus('//' + window.document.location.host)
  socket.on('error', function(error) { console.error(error) })
  var login = function() {
    socket.send(
      'xmpp.login.anonymous',
      { jid: '@anonymous.localhost' }
    )
    socket.on('xmpp.connection', function(data) {
      console.log('Connected as', data.jid)
      /* subscribeToNode() // Not implemented yet */
    })
  }
  socket.on('open', function() {
```

```
    console.log('Connected')
    login()
  })
  socket.on('timeout', function(reason) {
    console.error('Connection failed: ' + reason)
  })
  socket.on('end', function() {
    console.log('Socket connection closed')
    socket = null
  })
  socket.on('xmpp.error', function(error) {
    console.error('XMPP-FTW error', error)
  })
})
```

# Subscribing to a node

Next, we need to subscribe to the node where the stock data is being held so that we can retrieve (and get pushed) results. In xmpp-ftw, this is done using the xmpp.pubsub.subscribe event. As we know the server and the node, this makes the request quite simple (of course, we could always run a set of DISCO queries to find it too!).

In our login function, once logged in, we'll implement the subscribeToNode function:

```
var subscribeToNode = function() {
  var options = {
      node: 'stock-data-btc-rules',
      to: 'pubsub.localhost'
  }
  socket.send('xmpp.pubsub.subscribe', options, function(error, success)
  {
      if (error) return console.log('Error subscribing', error)
        getOlderPosts()
  })
}
```

In this code, we're requesting to subscribe to the node stock-data-btc-rules on the domain pubsub.localhost (strangely, the node we were publishing to earlier!). If there is an error in subscribing, then in the event callback, the variable error will be populated; we would report this to the console and progress no further. If we don't have an error then, the success variable will be populated. In this case, we aren't really concerned with its contents and just want to get on with the next step (retrieving some older data), but an example response looks something like the following:

```
{"subscription": "subscribed" }
```

# Retrieving historical results

The next step is to pull two pages of historical results from the `pubsub` node and then write these to a chart before we start publishing real-time data to it.

We'll add a function to our code to retrieve a page of existing items:

```
var items = []
var getOlderPosts = function() {
  var details = {
    node: 'stock-data-btc-rules',
    to: 'pubsub.localhost'
  }
  socket.send(
    'xmpp.pubsub.retrieve',
    details,
    function(error, posts) {
      if (error) return console.log('Error retrieving posts', error)
      posts.forEach(function(post) {
          items.push(post)
      })
      /* drawInitialChart() // Not implemented yet */
    }
  )
}
```

In this code, we simply ask for items from the `pubsub` node and Prosody will deliver us a set of results. In more advanced code, we can use **Result Set Management (RSM),** which would allow us to page through historical results for users to see, or restrict the number of historical results we retrieve.

We can inspect the items that come back to see what format they take. Here's a quick example:

```
[
  {
    entry: {
      json: {
        change: -2, timestamp: "2015-11-09T23:21:12.835Z",
        value: 502
      },
      id: "2015-11-09T23:21:12.835Z"
  },
  {
    entry: {
      json: {
        change: 4, timestamp: "2015-11-09T23:21:10.824Z",
```

```
      value: 506
    },
    id: "2015-11-09T23:21:10.824Z"
  }
]
```

To draw our chart, we'll now need to load up Smoothie charts and write our existing data to them. Once we have them, we can start adding real-time data, but let's not get ahead of ourselves. Here is the code for drawing the chart:

```
var stockChart = new TimeSeries()
var drawInitialChart = function() {
  var chart = new SmoothieChart()
  chart.addTimeSeries (
    stockChart,
    {
      strokeStyle: 'rgba(0, 255, 0, 1)',
      fillStyle: 'rgba(0, 255, 0, 0.2)',
      lineWidth: 4
    }
  )
  items.reverse().forEach(function(item) {
    stockChart.append(
      new Date(item.entry.json.timestamp).getTime(),
      item.entry.json.value
    )
  })
  chart.streamTo(document.getElementById('chart'), 250)
  /* letsGetReal-time() // Not implemented yet */
}
```

# Getting real-time

The last stage in our code is to start publishing our real-time stock updates. We're going to implement the `letsGetRealtime()` function. All this function really needs to do is send a presence stanza to the `pubsub` server to say that we're online. We'll also need to register a listener for `pubsub` push events and then add them to the charts.

Let's first write the code that sends the presence stanza:

```
var letsGetRealtime = function() {
  socket.send('xmpp.presence', { to: 'pubsub.localhost' })
}
```

That's it! Since presence isn't an IQ type stanza, we don't need to wait for a response, and we can now get on with handling our pushed data:

```
socket.on('xmpp.pubsub.push.item', function(item) {
  stockChart.append(
    new Date(item.entry.json.timestamp).getTime(),
    item.entry.json.value
  )
})
```

In the payload, we are also given details about where (that is, which domain) the payload came from and from, which node. In a production system, depending on our setup we might want to check the source of the data or even handle multiple incoming real-time feeds.

If we now fire up both the publisher code and the client code, we should be able to open a browser and see some glorious real-time charts!

```
node publisher & ./run.sh
```

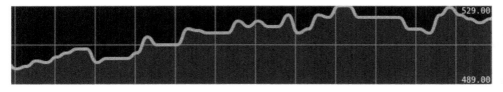

# Taking things further

In the preceding code, we used our XMPP server to publish real-time data to a `pubsub` node, connected as a client from a website, retrieved some historical data, and then received pushed updates (no server polling!).

Once the basic concepts here are understood, we can take things much further with little effort by leveraging more of XMPP. For example, we could update from multiple nodes and subscribe/unsubscribe whilst on a page to different pieces of real-time data while on another page. And how would we know about this data? Well, we'd run a DISCO#items query against the server to get a list. But what if we wanted to find out about the data each node held? Then we'd run a DISCO#info query against it and find out the information such a description, what data format it used, and when it was last updated.

With no changes to our code at all, we could also subscribe to nodes on remote servers and start getting pushed updates from those too (although generally we prevent anonymous users from making S2S requests to prevent spam).

By using RSM, we could page backwards in time to look at older posts and, staying with the stocks, look at the historical share price over a much longer period.

# Summary

In this chapter, we learned the basics of publish/subscribe in XMPP. While the premise of pubsub may be rather simple conceptually, it's a very powerful tool upon which many systems covering a huge range of functionality can be built, from social networks to fully federated database systems.

Once we learned about the basics, we went on to take a simple static website and add real-time data to it (well, in the form of made up stock values). To achieve this, we built a publishing client that generated data for us (imagine we were pulling data from RSS feeds, Twitter, or other constantly updating systems!) and published it to a pubsub node.

Once the publisher was completed in a small number of lines of JavaScript, we built a browser-based client that retrieved old data, wrote it to a graph, and then started receiving real-time updates from the server as data was being published.

There are several standard features of XMPP related to pubsub that we did not cover in this chapter. As always with XMPP, the best source of knowledge is to read the XEP documents, but hopefully you've seen enough to show you the power and versatility of the specification.

Now repeat after me: The whole world is a big giant pubsub system!

In the next chapter, we will look at developing XMPP components, which are server-side capabilities that act as plugins to the server.

# 7
# Creating an XMPP Component

If you're ever going to build custom functionality or implement your own business logic on top of existing XMPP standards, arguably the best way to do it is by creating a component. XMPP components are software modules that run on the server side but do not require modification of the server itself. This means you can easily update or upgrade your XMPP server without your own code getting in the way. You can also easily move components to other servers. And when writing your own component, there isn't even a need to implement it in the same language as your server!

The specifications for components are laid out in **XEP-0114** (`http://xmpp.org/extensions /xep-114.html`), which covers the connection flow for a component.

In this chapter, we'll learn how components connect with servers, and then delve straight into building a very simple component that is able to respond to `DISCO` requests and pings and can echo messages back to the user.

## Connection flow for components

The rather simple connection flow for a component is as follows: once a connection is established between the component and the XMPP server, the component sends the following stream opening:

```
<stream:stream
    xmlns='jabber:component:accept'
    xmlns:stream='http://etherx.jabber.org/streams'
    to='component.mcfly.fam'>
```

Note that the `to` address is the address that the component would like to be called with once it is attached to the server. It is not the address of the XMPP server (which would be `mcfly.fam`) as you might expect.

Once the server receives this stream opener and knows that it is configured for a component on this address, it responds with another stream, as follows:

```
<stream:stream xmlns:stream='http://etherx.jabber.org/streams'
    xmlns='jabber:component:accept' id='88mph'
    from='component.mcfly.fam'>
```

In order to prove their identity, components make use of a simple pre-shared string. This is combined with the stream ID sent with the server's opening stream element in order to form a handshake, which is sent for the server to authenticate.

This may seem like weak security when compared to the **Simple Authentication and Security Layer** (**SASL**) mechanisms used by XMPP clients, but the reason for this is that server administrators are generally in charge of running the components so they can lock connections down to certain IP/port combinations, or indeed, just to local interfaces. Therefore, it is acceptable to use a simple shared secret in this case.

The handshake value is calculated as follows:

1. Concatenate the server's stream ID with the shared secret.
2. Take the SHA-1 of the concatenated string.
3. Return the lowercase hexadecimal representation of the hash.

This value is then sent by the component in a handshake element for checking by the server:

```
<handshake>cf23df269e3eba035e633b207d99a74fbe165d94</handshake>
```

If the server is happy with the value it receives, it will respond with an empty handshake element. Otherwise, the component will receive a stream error and the connection will be closed:

```
<handshake/>
```

At this point, the component is connected and able to send and receive stanzas.

 Who are you? One security consideration to make when using components is that they are able to send stanzas on behalf of the server, so a `pretend.mcfly.fam` component could legally send a stanza as `marty@mcfly.fam`. Therefore, it is important that any component run from your server is trusted.

# Configuring a component in Prosody

To start working on our first XMPP component, we will first need to configure Prosody to listen for and interact with a component.

Open up the Prosody configuration file (In Ubuntu, this is in `/etc/prosody/prosody.cfg.lua`) and add the following lines:

```
Component "component.localhost"
    component_secret = "mysecretcomponentpassword"
```

By default, Prosody will only listen on `localhost` on port `5347`. This can be changed by adding configuration at the global level, such as in the following lines:

```
component_ports = { 5347 }
component_interface = "192.168.0.10"
```

After you update the configuration file, restart the XMPP server and confirm that Prosody is listening on the expected port by using telnet and observing the responses you get from the server:

```
lloyd@zenbook:~$ telnet localhost 5347
Trying 127.0.0.1...
Connected to localhost.
Escape character is '^]'.
bye!
<?xml version='1.0'?><stream:stream id='' xmlns:stream='http://etherx.jabber.org
/streams' version='1.0' xmlns='jabber:component:accept'><stream:error><not-well-
formed xmlns='urn:ietf:params:xml:ns:xmpp-streams'/></stream:error></stream:stre
am>Connection closed by foreign host.
```

And, if you type `telnet localhost:5347` and send a properly formed stream opener (in the following example, `<stream:stream xmlns='jabber:component:accept'` `xmlns:stream='http://etherx.jabber.org/streams'to='component.localhost'` `>`) you will see a response with the stream ID filled in:

```
dmkoelle@ubuntu:/etc/prosody$ telnet localhost 5347
Trying 127.0.0.1...
Connected to localhost.
Escape character is '^]'.
<stream:stream xmlns='jabber:component:accept' xmlns:stream='http://etherx.jabber.org/streams' t
o="component.localhost">
<?xml version='1.0'?><stream:stream id='80a10aa4-3be5-4a31-b32d-73bbba6b6cac' xmlns:stream='http
://etherx.jabber.org/streams' from='component.localhost' xmlns='jabber:component:accept'>
```

# Building our first XMPP component

As part of the `node-xmpp` suite of modules, there is a piece that allows the development of XMPP components, imaginatively named `node-xmpp-component`. We'll now use this to start building our first component.

The source code can be found on GitHub at `https://github.com/node-xmpp/node-xmpp/tree/master/packages/node-xmpp-component`, with usage examples found under the examples folder.

To get started, we'll create a new project folder and install the module from NPM:

```
cd ~
mkdir first-component
cd first-component
npm i node-xmpp-component
```

# Creating a component and connecting it to the server

Now we will create a new component to extend the capabilities of our existing server. In the first-component folder, create a file named `index.js`.

To connect the component to the server, we need to provide the module with connection settings, including the JID, we wish to use and the shared secret. As we haven't set up DNS, we will also need to specify the host server.

Add the following lines to `index.js`:

```
const Component = require('node-xmpp-component')
const component = new Component({
    jid: 'component.localhost',
    password: 'mysecretcomponentpassword',
    host: 'localhost',
    port: '5347'
})

component.on('online', () => console.log('Connected...') )
```

At this point, you have a component that can connect to the server. Go ahead and run your new component; and see that it connects to the XMPP server. Once the component is connected to the server, aside from handling errors, there are only two pieces of functionality that we need to implement: receiving a stanza and sending a stanza.

In the following sections, we will look at building a component to respond to DISCO requests and echo back chat messages to the sender, much like we did in earlier chapters.

# Receiving a stanza and responding to a DISCO#info query

The way a component receives a stanza is similar to how a client receives a stanza by using the on function and looking specifically for a stanza, as follows:

```
component.on('stanza', (stanza) => {
console.log('Stanza received! ')
console.log(stanza)
}
```

Remember that the stanza can be a presence, message, or iq stanza. One of the first stanzas you want to listen for in your component is an iq stanza. When your component is connected to the server, the server will attempt to get DISCO#info information from the component to find out what services the component provides. It's important to implement a response to DISCO#info; let's put that in place.

First, replace the preceding code with the following code:

```
component.on('stanza', (stanza) => {
    if (true === stanza.is('iq')) {
    handleIq(stanza)
    }
})
```

Next, we will create the handleIq function. In this function, we first need to make sure that there is a query associated with the iq stanza. If there is, and if the request is indeed asking for DISCO#info, the component must respond with a new stanza that describes the identity and features of the component. Keep in mind that the recipient of this stanza will be the sender of the request, and the sender of this stanza is the component itself, so we can use the to/from values that we are receiving from the message as the from/to values in our reply.

Since we're creating a stanza in this code, please also add `Stanza = require('node-xmpp-component').Stanza` to the beginning of `index.js`:

```
const handleIq = (stanza) => {
    const query = stanza.getChild('query')
    if (!query)
    return
    if (query.attrs.xmlns === 'http://jabber.org/protocol/disco#info')
    {
      const reply = new Stanza('iq', {
        type: 'result',
        id: stanza.id,
        from: stanza.to,
        to: stanza.from
      })
        .c('query', { xmlns: 'http://jabber.org/protocol/disco#info' })
        .c('identity', {
          category: 'chat',
          name: 'First Component',
          type: 'text'
        })
        .c('feature', {
          var: 'http://jabber.org/protocol/chat'
        })

    component.send(reply)
    console.log("Replying with " + stanza)
    }
}
```

Now the component is capable of responding to a `DISCO#info` request. In this case, our component is letting clients know that it provides a chat capability. The response also gives a name to the component.

# Responding to a chat message

The component that we are building will be listening for chat messages, and it will echo those chat messages back to the client. Using the same `component.on('stanza')` function that we implemented before, we can delegate to a `handleMessage` function if the incoming stanza is of type `message`. Modify your `component.on('stanza')` to the following:

```
component.on('stanza', function(stanza) {
    if (true === stanza.is('iq')) {
    handleIq(stanza);
    }
```

```
        else if (true === stanza.is('message')) {
        handleMessage(stanza)
        }
    } )
```

Now that you are experienced in implementing a response to a DISCO#info request, you will probably find the response to a chat message to follow a familiar structure. We want to create a new stanza, again using the to/from of the sender as the from/to of our response, and we simply want to respond with the same message that we received.

Here is the handleMessage function:

```
const handleMessage = function(stanza) {
    if (stanza.attrs.type === 'chat') {
    console.log('Responding to chat message by sending that same message
back to the client')
    var text = stanza.getChild('body').getText()
    var reply = new Stanza('message', {
        to: stanza.from,
        from: stanza.to,
        type: 'chat'
    } ).c('body').t(text)
    component.send(reply);
    }
}
```

Once you implement this function, you will have a component that responds to DISCO#info requests and chat messages! Let's create a client that connects to the component and can start chatting and we can start chatting.

# Creating a client that connects to the component

To make the separation between the component and the client clear, let's start a new project. We will also need to install node-xmpp-client into this new project:

```
cd ~
mkdir client-using-first-component
cd client-using-first-component
npm i node-xmpp-client
```

In your ~/client-using-first-component folder, create a file called client.js.

The client will connect to the component and it will send a chat message after it successfully connects. We can connect using the same bot credentials that were introduced earlier. Notice we are connecting to `localhost` itself as the server, as opposed to the component's Jabber ID. We will use the component's `jid` in just a bit to send messages directly to the component, but to create a connection; we just need to specify the server.

Enter the following code into `client.js`:

```
var Client = require('node-xmpp-client')

var options = {
    jid: 'bot@localhost',
    password: 'tellnoone',
    host: 'localhost'
}

var client = new Client(options)
client.on('online', function(connectionDetails) {
    console.log('Client is connected!')
    console.log(connectionDetails)
})
```

Once you are connected to the server, you will want to start sending messages to the component. Recall that when we created the component, we provided a Jabber ID for the component itself: `component.localhost`. When sending messages to the component, we'll need to use that same `jid` in the `to` value of our stanza.

To test the full life cycle of the component, the first message that we want to send to the component is a `DISCO#info` request. Then, we should send a presence message to make the presence of our client known. After that, we can send a chat message and expect to receive the same message repeated back.

We are going to create a function called `sendMessages()` to send these three messages after receiving notice of the successful connection, so in the code you entered previously, add a call to `sendMessages()` just after `console.log(connectionDetails)`.

Here is the `sendMessages()` function, which generates an `iq` stanza, a presence stanza (simply a `<presence/>` tag), and a message stanza containing a chat message:

```
const sendMessages = function() {
    var iqMessage = new Stanza('iq', {
        type: 'get',
        id: 'query1',
        to: 'component.localhost'
    }).c('query', { xmlns: 'http://jabber.org/protocol/disco#info'
```

```
  })
    client.send(iqMessage)
    client.send('<presence/>')

    var message = new Stanza('message', {
      to: 'component.localhost',
      type: 'chat'
    } )
    message.c('body').t('Hello, Component!')
    client.send(message)
}
```

Notice that the chat message will be directed to component.localhost. This will ensure that our new component will hear the message.

Since we are awaiting a response from the component, we will want to add one more method to the client, something that shows us when the chat message is echoed back. Let's be sure to listen for incoming stanzas by adding the following code to client.js:

```
client.on('stanza', function(stanza) {
    if (stanza.is('message') && stanza.attrs.type == 'chat') {
    console.log('Received message: ' + stanza.getChild('body').getText())
    }
} )
```

So now, in addition to having a component that responds to chat messages by echoing them back to the sender, we have a client that sends chat messages to the component and awaits the echoed message. Let's run these and see how they work!

# Running your new component and client

First, ensure that your Prosody service is running with the configurations indicated earlier in this chapter.

We are going to run the component and client in two separate terminal windows. Open one terminal window, go to your first-component folder, and start the component:

```
cd ~/first-component
node index.js
```

Open a second terminal window, go to the folder in which we placed the client, and start the client:

```
cd ~/client-using-first-component
node client.js
```

Once you run the client, you will see console output in both terminal windows showing that the communication is taking place. In the client window, the final line of console output that you will see should be:

```
Received message: Hello, Component!
```

This message is a confirmation that the **Hello, Component!** chat message originally sent from the client has been echoed back by our new component.

Congratulations! Of course, a **Hello, Component** message only scratches the surface of what interesting things we can do with this capability. In the upcoming chapters, we will create components that are a bit more interesting!

```
dmkoelle@ubuntu: ~/first-component
dmkoelle@ubuntu:~/first-component$ node index.js
Connected...
Replying with <iq type="get" to="component.localhost" from="bot@localhost/4331f132-
12c6-4756-b134-3f4dd960679a" id="query1" xmlns:stream="http://etherx.jabber.org/str
eams"><query xmlns="http://jabber.org/protocol/disco#info"/></iq>
Responding to chat message by sending that same message back to the client
```

```
dmkoelle@ubuntu: ~/client-using-first-component
dmkoelle@ubuntu:~/client-using-first-component$ node client.js
Client is connected!
{ jid:
   { _local: 'bot',
     user: 'bot',
     _domain: 'localhost',
     _resource: '4331f132-12c6-4756-b134-3f4dd960679a' } }
Received message: Hello, Component!
```

Running the component (back terminal) and client (front terminal)

# Summary

In this chapter, you learned what an XMPP component is, how it augments the capabilities provided by the server, and how the separation between the server and the component is useful from a configuration management perspective.

You learned how to create both an XMPP component and a client that connects and shares information with the component.

In the next chapter, we'll create a component that provides an interesting capability to our server; it will allow for the creation of a collaborative whiteboard, which co-workers across large distances can use to share visual ideas with each other.

# 8

# Building a Basic XMPP-Based Pong Game

In this chapter, we will build an implementation of the classic game **Pong**, using XMPP chat messages to communicate the position of the paddles and ball between clients. The game will be based on the XMPP-FTW skeleton and will draw to an HTML canvas. The intention of this chapter is to illustrate one way in which you could use XMPP to power your own user-centered applications. Specifically, in this chapter we take a very basic approach of sending application updates via the body of basic chat messages. In the next chapter, we will take a different approach of creating our own messages to share between the client and a custom server component which we will build; the approach taken in this chapter is to teach you how to build an application (ok, game) on XMPP using its core functionality before we extend things later.

Why base this demonstration on Pong? For one thing, Pong uses basic visualizations, so we can focus on the XMPP communication rather than details about the user interface.

We will continue to build on this example in the following chapter, in which we will complete the XMPP Pong game with a server-side component to handle the game logic rather than allowing the clients to enforce it themselves. The next chapter will also introduce an XMPP-FTW extension that allows our clients to exchange messages with application specific XML payloads, rather than the approach taken in this chapter, in which we use the body of the messages to share game state.

# Overview of Basic XMPP Pong

With the idea of keeping the end in mind as we get started, *Figure 1* shows a picture of our final client-side application. The interaction is, hopefully, intuitive: the player can move their paddle up or down by clicking and dragging the mouse and the ball bounces off the paddles and off the top and bottom walls. If the ball passes a player's paddle, the other player wins a point:

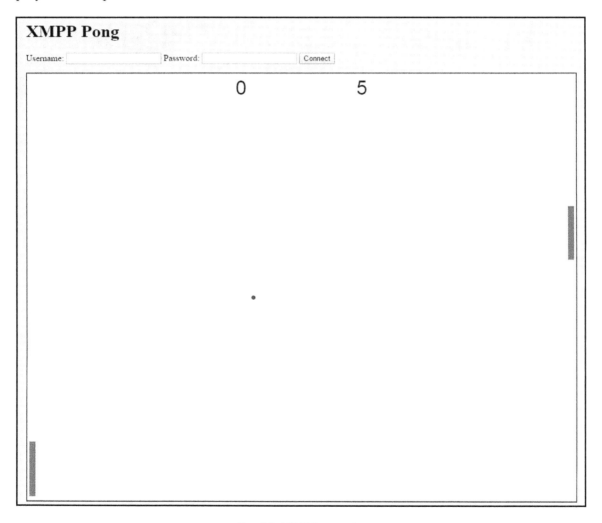

Figure 1. Basic XMPP Pong screenshot

As a player moves their paddle, XMPP messages will be sent to the other player and the graphics will be updated in the other player's game. Each player's client code will maintain the ball state, which is clearly not an ideal way to run a game.

Since a player can move their own paddle by moving the mouse, and the opposing player's paddle would be moved by an incoming XMPP message to the first player's client, there are two ways for the paddles to be updated on the screen, so we'll need to keep that in mind as we develop this client. In our game, the current player's paddle will appear on the left, and the opponent's paddle will appear on the right. This means that the two players will see games that are mirror images of each other. When we get to Chapter 9, *Enhancing XMPPong with a Server Component and Custom Messages* and introduce a server-side component, we will rectify that, but for now, in your own client view, you get to move the paddle on the left.

Let's start this chapter by developing the client view itself, so we can build the picture you see in Figure 1. After that, we'll walk through adding XMPP capabilities to the game.

# Getting Started

To start, we will use XMPP-FTW to create a skeleton for our project. Recall that we did this in Chapter 5, *Building a Multi-User Chat Application* as well:

```
cd ~
git clone git@github.com:xmpp-ftw/skeleton-project.git pong
cd pong
```

Now we're going to jump right into the client code.

# Developing the HTML canvas

Let's start by creating an HTML canvas in which the game will take place. The HTML for our code belongs in `~/pong/views/index.ejs`. You'll find an existing `index.ejs` file there from the skeleton you just cloned. We will replace the contents of `index.ejs` with the following code.

We want to write a simple page that creates an HTML5 canvas element. The logic that drives the canvas will be placed in the `pong.js` file we're about to write. Enter the following code into `index.ejs`:

```
<!DOCTYPE html>
<html>
  <head>
  <title>XMPP Pong</title>
  <style type="text/css">
    body { background-color: #eee; }
    #container { margin:0 auto; width: 640px; }
    #pong { border: 1px solid; background-color: #fff; }
  </style>
  </head>
  <body>
      <div id="container">
      <h1>XMPP Pong </h1>
        <!-- More to be filled in here soon! -->
          <canvas id="pong" width="1000" height="800" tabindex="1">
            <p>This browser does not support the HTML5 Canvas element.</p>
          </canvas>
        </div>
        <script src="http://code.jquery.com/jquery-1.11.0.min.js"></script>
          <script src="/scripts/primus.js"></script>
          <script src="/scripts/pong.js"></script>
  </body>
</html>
```

We will also start writing `pong.js`. As a script, this file belongs in `~/pong/public/scripts`. For starters, we'll just create a shell that gets the canvas ready to be drawn on. We will populate the rest of this file as we go. Initially, let's put in the following pieces:

- Getting an animation frame and setting up the initial game loop
- Declaring the variables we'll need
- Creating an `init()` function, which will set up the game variables

Here is the initial content of `pong.js`, and it uses the jQuery ready function at the beginning of the code to know when the webpage has loaded:

```
$(window.document).ready(function() {
// Global variables
var GAME_WIDTH = 1000
var GAME_HEIGHT = 800
var PAD_X_MARGIN = 5
var PAD_THICKNESS = 10
```

```
var BALL_RADIUS = 3
var BALL_X_SPEED = 4

// Player variables
var pad1Height = 100, pad2Height = 100
var pad1Y = (GAME_HEIGHT - pad1Height) / 2, pad2Y = (GAME_HEIGHT -
pad2Height) / 2
var ballX, ballY
var ballDeltaX, ballDeltaY
var score1, score2
var mouseDown = false
var opponentJid
var gameOn = false
```

Now, let's add some variables and functionality that will allow us to draw the game of XMPPong to the page. The game loop will allow the XMPPong game to be animated:

```
//Drawing variables
var canvas = document.getElementById('pong')
var context = canvas.getContext('2d')

function init() {
// Prevent I-Beam cursor from appearing on mousedown
   canvas.onselectstart = function () { return false; }
}
function gameLoop(canvas, context) {
// We will populate this with update and drawing functions
  requestAnimFrame(function() {
    requestAnimFrame(function() {
    gameLoop(canvas, context)
  });
}
  init()
  gameloop()
})
```

The preceding code gives us a framework to work with. Now, let's complete the picture a little more, first by using the mouse to move the paddles, then with the code to draw everything to the screen and update the ball position.

# Adding the mouse listeners for moving the paddle

Let's start adding the ability to move the paddles using the mouse. To move a paddle, the user will click and drag on the image of the paddle. We will need three listeners, since we need to know when the mouse button is pressed, when it is released, and when the mouse is moved.

Add the following listeners to `init` function in `pong.js`:

```
canvas.addEventListener('mousedown', doMouseDownEvent, false);
canvas.addEventListener('mouseup', doMouseUpEvent, false);
canvas.addEventListener('mousemove', doMouseMoveEvent, false);
```

Now let's add the `mouse` functions. When the user presses the mouse button, we want to set a flag that indicates the paddle is moving. We'll call this `mouseDown`, and we already have it in our member variables. We also need to know the location of the mouse when the button is pressed. Eventually, we will need to send the new position to the other player. When the player lifts the mouse button, we will clear `mouseDown`. If the user moves the mouse while `mouseDown` is true, we will know to update the paddle position.

The code following segment shows the mouse event functions. We'll also create a separate function to specifically set the paddle position, since we want to call that when the user clicks on the screen and when they drag the mouse

```
function doMouseDownEvent(event) {
  mouseDown = true;
  setPad1Position(event.layerY)
}

function doMouseUpEvent(event) {
  mouseDown = false
}

function doMouseMoveEvent(event) {
  if (mouseDown) {
    setPad1Position(event.layerY)
  }
}

function setPad1Position(candidateY) {
  if ((candidateY> 0) && (candidateY<GAME_HEIGHT)) {
    pad1Y = candidateY
  }
}
```

We now have a paddle that can move vertically, and that is limited to move only within the bounds of the game space (as indicated by the bounds checking code in `setPad1Position`). It would be nice to see this in action, so next we will implement the drawing code.

# Drawing and updating the game

To draw to the screen, we will use the age-old animation principal of first clearing everything in the game space, then drawing each of the elements. The elements consists of the ball, the left and right side paddles the score:

```
function clearField() {
  context.fillStyle = "#FFFFFF"
  context.fillRect(0, 0, GAME_WIDTH, GAME_HEIGHT)
  context.strokeStyle = "#000000"
  context.strokeRect(0, 0, GAME_WIDTH, GAME_HEIGHT)
}
function drawBall() {
  context.beginPath()
  context.arc(ballX, ballY, BALL_RADIUS, 0, Math.PI * 2, false)
  context.fillStyle = "#C11B17"
  context.fill()
  context.strokeStyle = "#9F000F"
  context.stroke();
}
function drawPad(x, y, w, h) {
  context.fillStyle = "#306EFF"
  context.fillRect(x, y, w, h)
  context.strokeStyle = "#2B65EC"
  context.strokeRect(x, y, w, h)
}
function drawPad1() {
  drawPad(PAD_X_MARGIN, pad1Y, PAD_THICKNESS, pad1Height)
}
function drawPad2() {
  drawPad(GAME_WIDTH - PAD_X_MARGIN - PAD_THICKNESS, pad2Y, PAD_THICKNESS,
pad2Height);
}
function drawScore() {
  context.font = "36px Arial";
  context.fillStyle = "#000000";
  context.fillText(score1, GAME_WIDTH / 2 - 100 -
    context.measureText(score1).width, 40);
  context.fillText(score2, GAME_WIDTH / 2 + 100, 40);
}
```

Now let's fill in the game logic and the game loop itself. As the game is played, we want to update the ball position based on the direction of the ball (indicated by our ballDeltaX and ballDeltaY variables), and we want the ball to bounce off paddles or the top and bottom walls. To achieve this, we will implement the following functions:

```
function resetBallLocationAndDelta(deltaX, deltaY) {
  ballX = GAME_WIDTH / 2
  ballY = GAME_HEIGHT / 2
  ballDeltaX = deltaX
  ballDeltaY = deltaY
}
function updateBallPosition() {
  ballX += ballDeltaX
  ballY += ballDeltaY
  if (ballX - BALL_RADIUS < PAD_X_MARGIN) {
  // Did ball get past Player 1?
  score2 += 1
  resetBallLocationAndDelta(-BALL_X_SPEED, -1)
}
  else if (ballX + BALL_RADIUS > GAME_WIDTH - PAD_X_MARGIN) {
  //Did ball get past Player 2?
  score1 += 1
  resetBallLocationAndDelta(+BALL_X_SPEED, -1)
}
// Test for ricochet on top and bottom of game
  if ((ballY - BALL_RADIUS <= 0) || (ballY + BALL_RADIUS >= GAME_HEIGHT)) {
    ballDeltaY = -ballDeltaY
  }
// Test for ricochet on paddles
if (
    (ballX - BALL_RADIUS <= PAD_X_MARGIN + PAD_THICKNESS) &&
    (ballY + BALL_RADIUS >= pad1Y) &&
    (ballY - BALL_RADIUS <= pad1Y + pad1Height)
  ) {
      ballDeltaX = -ballDeltaX
      ballDeltaY = -ballDeltaY
    }
    else if (
      (ballX + BALL_RADIUS >= GAME_WIDTH - PAD_X_MARGIN - PAD_THICKNESS)
      && (ballY + BALL_RADIUS >= pad1Y) &&
      (ballY - BALL_RADIUS <= pad1Y + pad1Height))
    {
      ballDeltaX = -ballDeltaX
      ballDeltaY = -ballDeltaY;
    }
  }
}
```

Now let's add calls to these functions in the game loop itself:

```
function gameLoop(canvas, context) {
  if (gameOn) {
    updateBallPosition()
    clearField()
    drawPad1()
    drawPad2()
    drawBall(ballX, ballY)
    drawScore()
  }
  requestAnimFrame(function() {
    gameLoop(canvas, context)
  });
}
```

Finally, get the ball rolling by adding the following line to `init()`:

```
resetBallLocationAndDelta(-BALL_X_SPEED, +1)
```

At this point, you have the first half of a Pong game. You can play it if you'd like (if you override the default value of the `gameOn` variable to be true), but you can only move the left paddle. Once you move the paddle to hit the ball, there is no one on the other end to hit the ball back to you. You will win every game! To save you from so much winning, let's now move on to the part of the code that will send XMPP messages to the other client, and respond to messages from the other client.

# Sending and receiving XMPP messages in Pong

There are several places where we want to send and receive XMPP messages in Pong. We first need a message so that each player knows who the other player is. Then we need to send messages when the player moves the position of the left-side pad (from their perspective), and we need to receive messages from the opponent to know how to move the right-side pad when our opponent moves their mouse.

# Sending and receiving a Hello message

The first thing the client needs to do is create a connection, then send a Hello message, so that the opponent player. This will let us populate the `opponentJid` member variable, so we have someone to play against and address the paddle updates to. The `connect` function will be called when we press the button on the webpage to connect, and it will call the `sendHello` function:

```
window.connect = function() {
    var options = {
        jid: document.getElementById('username').value,
        password: document.getElementById('password').value
    }
  socket.send('xmpp.login', options)
  socket.once('xmpp.connection', function(connectionDetails) {
      console.log(options.jid + ' is connected!')
      console.log(connectionDetails)
      var jid = connectionDetails.jid.user + '@' +
        onnectionDetails.jid.domain + '/' + connectionDetails.jid.resource
      alert('You are connected as ' + jid +
        ' you can share this JID with an opponent to set up a game')
      sendHello(document.getElementById('opponent').value)
  })
}

  function sendHello(opponentJid) {
    socket.send(
      'xmpp.chat.message',
      {
        to: opponentJid,
        content: 'hello'
      }
    )
    console.log('Sent Hello message to', opponentJid)
  }
```

We also need to handle this message when it comes in, so we will introduce our `handleMessage` function and start by handling the Hello message. In the next section, we'll use the same function to handle paddle updates as well:

```
function handleMessage(data) {
  if (0 === data.content.indexOf('hello')) {
    opponentJid = data.from.local + '@' + data.from.domain +
      '/' + data.from.resource
   console.log('Received hello from ', opponentJid)
   gameOn = true
```

```
    }
  }
```

Now, we need one more thing in place. What's going to call `handleMessage`? That's right, we need to create a socket object and tell the socket what to do in response to various XMPP messages that the socket may receive. We'll use `primus` here, so make sure you also have `primus.js` in your public/scripts folder. Add the following code; a good place for this is just beneath the declaration of the variables near the top of your `pong.js` file:

```
var socket = new Primus('//' + window.document.location.host)
  socket.on('error', function(error) { console.error(error) })
  socket.on('open', function() {
    console.log('Connected')
  })
  socket.on('timeout', function(reason) {
    console.error('Connection failed: ' + reason)
  })
  socket.on('end', function() {
    console.log('Socket connection closed')
    socket = null
  })
  socket.on('xmpp.error', function(error) {
    console.error('XMPP-FTW error', error)
  })
  socket.on('xmpp.error.client', function(error) {
    console.error('XMPP-FTW client error', error)
  })
  socket.on('xmpp.chat.message', handleMessage)
  socket.on('xmpp.discover.client', handleDisco)
```

# Sending a paddle update

To send paddle updates, we will create a new function, `sendPaddleUpdate()`, which will create a message with the updated information and send it:

```
function sendPaddleUpdate(newPadY) {
  socket.send(
    'xmpp.chat.message',
    {
      to: opponentJid,
      content: 'paddleUpdate:' + newPadY
    }
  )
  console.log('Sent update - newPadY = ', newPadY)
}
```

Now we need to call this function when the left paddle's position is changed. Find the `setPad1Position()` function. Just after setting `pad1Y` to `candidateY`, insert a call to `sendPaddleUpdate(pad1Y)`:

```
function setPad1Position(candidateY) {
  if ((candidateY > 0) && (candidateY < GAME_HEIGHT)) {
    pad1Y = candidateY
    sendPaddleUpdate(pad1Y)
  }
}
```

## Receiving a paddle update

In addition to sending our own paddle location, we need to react when the other client updates a paddle position. Using the `handleMessage` function, we just created to receive the "Hello" message, let's augment it to also watch for a `paddleUpdate` message. When the `paddleUpdate` message is received, this function will set the position of `pad2Y`:

```
function handleMessage(data) {
  if (0 === data.content.indexOf('hello')) {
    opponentJid = stanza.from.local + '@' + stanza.from.domain +
    '/' + stanza.from.resource
    console.log('Received hello from ', opponentJid)
    gameOn = true
  } else if (0 === data.content.indexOf('paddleUpdate')) {
    pad2Y = data.content.split(':')[1]
  }
}
```

## Connecting the clients

Our approach has been bottom-up rather than top-down: first we built the game, then we built the message handlers, and now it's time to bring in the client but all of the pieces are coming together. Next, we want to connect two players so that two people can play **XMPPong**! First, we need those two players to have unique JIDs, so we need to let each player log into the game.

First, we need to create some accounts so that multiple people can log into the game. Let's create accounts for two players, Marty and Jennifer:

```
sudo prosodyctl adduser marty@localhost
sudo prosodyctl adduser jennifer@localhost
```

For simplicity, I made Marty's password `m` and Jennifer's password `j`.

Next, we need to let Marty and Jennifer log into their respective Pong clients. We'll need to extend `index.ejs` with a couple of input fields to let our players enter their username and password, and we'll need to extend `pong.js` to accept the new username and password combination and use that to log into the chat server.

First, insert the following form into `index.ejs`. Put the following HTML code between the existing `</h1>` and `<canvas>` tags:

```
<p>
  <form>
    Username:
    <input type="text" id="username" required />
    Password:
    <input type="password" id="password" required />
    Opponent JID (ensure you enter your opponent's
      <strong>full JID</strong> here):
    <input type="text" id="opponent" reqwuired />
    <button type="button" onclick="connect()">Connect</button>
  </form>
</p>
```

Recall that we created the `connect()` function in earlier in this chapter.

We now have a fully functioning, `XMPP-backed Pong` client! Ready to test this out? First, run the application from `~/pong`:

```
node index.js
```

Now open one browser and log in as `marty@localhost`. Open a second browser and log in as `jennifer@localhost`. If you're fast enough to switch between browsers, you can adopt both personalities as you hit the ball back and forth with your paddle.

# Advertising the Pong feature of clients (Client DISCO)

One additional thing we should add to our XMPPong game is the ability for clients to discover it. Recall that a `DISCO#info` request to the server will list the features that the room supports.

To do that, let's but a handler in that recognizes when a `DISCO` request is being sent:

```
socket.on('xmpp.discover.client', handleDisco)
```

You can place that right next to `socket.on('xmpp.chat.message, handleMessage)`.

Now, we'll implement the `handleDisco` function, which will send the identity of this client and the features it supports:

```
function handleDisco(data) {
  socket.send(
    'xmpp.discover.client',
    {
      to: data.from,
      id: data.id,
      features: [
        { kind: 'identity', type: 'text', name: 'XMPPong',
          category: 'chat' },
        { kind: 'feature', var: 'http://jabber.org/protocol/chat' }
      ]
    },
    function(error, data) { console.log(error, data) }
  )
  console.log('Replied to disco#info request with ', reply)
}
```

Now our XMPPong game can respond to `DISCO#info` requests! You can try this out from your Empathy client.

# Issues with a basic implementation

Remember `bot@localhost`? Fire up Empathy and log in with the JID `bot@localhost` and password `tellnoone`. As Marty and Jennifer are passing the ball to each other, `bot@localhost` could send the hello message to either player an hijack a place in the game! While this might be interesting, this is not the kind of behavior we would hope to see in a more advanced application that uses XMPP. Instead, we would want to make sure someone like bot can't inject themselves into the game (I'll bet you could make bot change one of the player's paddle positions). We wouldn't want game control messages and chat messages to be shown in the same chat window although one thing we could do is enable chat in `XMPPong`

In the following chapter, we are going to address these issues. We will look into employing custom namespaces, creating a server-side component that can help prevent cheating. We will even keep track of wins and losses and create a leaderboard of the best players. For now, in this chapter, we have assembled the basics of getting a game up and running and using XMPP to share game messages back and forth.

Chances are, you are not going to implement Pong as part of your projects for fun or profit. Think of this as a simple example, which you can build on to power your own applications. Maybe it's a graph-drawing application or a whiteboard session where users see each other's drawing on the same canvas in real time. Maybe it's a music-composition application, or even a music-performance application, which lets people around the world work together to perform in front of a virtual audience through a multi-user chat (MUC) room. Maybe it's a system that lets autonomous software agents communicate in real time to perform chores around the IT department, with occasional input from their human counterparts to direct their work. Whatever creative and value-providing applications you can devise may start with your inspiration from XMPPong.

# Summary

The purpose of this chapter was to show you how you can set up a useful client-side application that uses XMPP to share messages across clients and you can challenge someone to a game of Pong!

In the following chapter, we will build on this example by creating a server-side component to manage the application state, and we will create our own XMPP-FTW extension that will allow us to craft our own messages rather than sending data through the text of a chat message.

# 9
# Enhancing XMPPong with a Server Component and Custom Messages

In Chapter 8, *Building a Basic XMPP-Based Pong Game* we created the basics of XMPPong. We took a lot of shortcuts to get a basic game up and running. In this chapter, we will continue what we left in earlier chapter to build the pong game, by creating an XMPP component to manage more aspects of the game. In the previous chapter, we relied on each client to manage a lot of information; the position of the ball, the position of the paddles, the score, and we left the game wide open for someone to inject other messages into the conversation and throw off the game.

In this chapter, our component will keep track of the game state and prevent cheating. We will introduce the use of an XMPP-FTW extension to allow us to create payloads of XML data that we can send through XMPP between the client and server component. The work we do in this chapter will prepare us for the next chapter, in which we talk about deploying XMPP applications to the real world.

## Designing the information flow for XMPPong

Having worked on a quick version of XMPPong in Chapter 8, *Building a Basic XMPP-Based Pong Game,* as we plan to engage in some more intense engineering of our solution in this chapter, let's take a moment to think about how we would like XMPPong to work.

First, we are going to create a server component that knows how to manage an XMPPong game. We will expect two players to be connected to the component through their own clients. We expect messages to be sent between the component and the clients. Naturally, the component will handle all of the game logic (or business logic if we weren't building a game!), and clients will handle the graphical output and report on input from the players.

In preparation for all of this, let's talk about the messages we expect to be sent between the controller and the clients.

1. The component will start, and it will contain settings that each client will need to conform to, in terms of the playing field size (width and height), initial paddle position, and initial ball position. We'll call these the default settings.

2. When a client connects with the component, the client will receive those default settings and set up its view appropriately.

3. The first client to check in will be Player 1. The second client will be Player 2. After that, the component will not accept a new player; in fact, it will return an error message if additional players attempt to join a game

4. When the player sitting at one of the clients moves their mouse to change the position of the paddle, the client will send a paddle update to the component.

5. The component must pass along one player's paddle update to the other player's client. That client needs to update the position of the opponent's paddle.

6. When the component moves the ball as it's handling the game logic, the component will send a ball update to both clients. The clients will need to update the position of the ball.

7. When a player misses the ball, the component will send a score update to both clients. The clients will need to update their display of the score.

8. When a player reaches 10 points, we'll consider the game to be over. Both clients will need to display a Game Over indicator.

These messages are summarized in Table:

| Message | Fields | Contents of `<message>` |
|---|---|---|
| `playerCheckingIn` *from* **client** *to* **component** | (none) | `<body> playercheckingin</body>`<br>` <pong xmlns="xmpp:game:pong" />`<br>`<action>playercheckingin</action> </pong>` |

| | | |
|---|---|---|
| dimensions *from* **component** *to* **client** | width, height, paddleWidth, paddleHeight, paddleMargin, paddleY, ballRadius, side | ```<body> dimensions</body>```<br>```<pong xmlns="xmpp:game:pong">```<br>```<action>dimensions</action>```<br>```<width>value</width>```<br>```<height>value</height>```<br>```<paddlewidth></paddlewidth>```<br>```<paddleheight>value</paddleheight>```<br>```<paddlemargin>val</paddlemargin>```<br>```<paddley>value</paddley>```<br>```<ballradius>value</ballradius>```<br>```<side>0 or 1</side>```<br>```</pong>``` |
| ballPosition from **component** to **client** | ballX, ballY | ```<body>ballPosition</body>```<br>```<pong xmlns="xmpp:game:pong">```<br>```<action>ballposition</action>```<br>```<x>value</x>```<br>```<y>value</y>```<br>```</pong>``` |
| scoreUpdate from **component** to **client** | player1score, player2score | ```<body> scoreUpdate</body>```<br>```<pong xmlns="xmpp:game:pong">```<br>```<action>scoreupdate</action>```<br>```<player1>score</player1>```<br>```<player2>score</player2>```<br>```</pong>``` |
| paddlePosition from **client** to **component** | paddleY | ```<body> paddlePosition</body>```<br>```<pong xmlns="xmpp:game:pong">```<br>```<action>paddleposition</action>```<br>```<y>value</y>```<br>```</pong>``` |
| opponentPaddleUpdate from **component** to **client** | paddleY | ```<body> opponentPaddlePosition</body>```<br>```<pong xmlns="xmpp:game:pong">```<br>```<action>opponentPaddleUpdate</action>```<br>```<y>value</y>```<br>```</pong>``` |
| gameOver from **component** to **client** | (none) | ```<body>gameOver</body>```<br>```<pong xmlns="xmpp:game:pong" />```<br>```<action>gameOver</action>```<br>```</pong>``` |

Sending our messages as we did in the previous chapter using core messaging functionality is far from idea. So we're now using a custom format sent via message stanzas. However, building XML in the browser is cumbersome (and let's face it would put most web developers off), so how do we make this integration easier? We build an XMPP-FTW extension of course!

The XMPP-FTW extension will allow us to create a script that knows how to parse our custom message format. It will also be able to build the appropriate message stanzas from simple JSON provided by the browser. We can send messages with a namespace like xmpp:pong, and write our own schema for the type of data that should exist within those messages. When the messages are parsed, they will construct the appropriate stanzas to send to the server component. We'll develop our extension soon enough; let's first look into how we're going to build that component, then we can create the extension that builds and parses the appropriate stanzas based on the content of the messages.

# Developing the XMPP component for XMPPong

As mentioned earlier, the server component for XMPPong will be concerned with managing key aspects of the game: owning the default settings, managing the position of the ball, keeping track of the client's paddle movements, and maintaining the score.

Let's start by editing the Prosody configuration to support the new XMPPong component . Add the following to the end of the prosody.cfg.lua file (In Ubuntu /etc/prosody/prosody.cfg.lua):

```
Component "xmppong.localhost"
  component_secret = "mysecretcomponentpassword"
```

Now let's create the component itself. To get started, create a new project folder and install the node-xmpp-component module:

```
cd ~
mkdir pong-component
cd pong-component
npm i node-xmpp-component
```

Navigate into the pong-component directory and create a new file called index.js. We're going to start the component with some boilerplate code:

```
//
// "XMPPong" Server-Side Component
//
const Component = require('node-xmpp-component')
    , ltx = require('ltx')
    , Gameloop = require('node-gameloop')
const componentJid = 'xmppong.localhost'
const PONG_NAMESPACE = 'xmpp:game:pong'
const component = new Component({
    componentJid,
    password: 'mysecretcomponentpassword',
    host: 'localhost',
    port: '5347'
})
component.on('online', () => console.log('Connected...'))
```

Now let's get straight into adding some functions to manage the game itself. First, we'll need all sorts of variables. Many of these will be similar to you based on work in the previous chapter. Please add the following lines to the component's index.js file:

```
// Playing field dimensions
const width = 800, height = 600
const playfieldMinX = 0, playfieldMinY = 0
const playfieldMaxX = playfieldMinX + width
const playfieldMaxY = playfieldMinY + height

// Paddle sizes
const paddleMargin = 10
const paddleWidth = 20
let paddleHeight = [100, 100]
let paddleY = [height / 2, height / 2]

// Ball data
let ballX, ballY
const ballRadius = 3
let ballHeading    // degrees
let ballSpeed      // pixels per millisecond
```

```
// Keeping track of players and their scores
const score = []
let playerJids = []

// Game state, so we know when the game starts and ends
// (0 = not started, 1 = started, 2 = finished)
let gameState
```

Now we're going to implement some functions specific to the game mechanics. We'll get to the messaging part soon, but for now let's get the game logic in place.

First, we want to keep track of when players check in. When a player checks in, the component will remember the player's JID. The component will also keep track of how many players in the game. Of course, we're looking for a total of two players to start the game. If additional clients attempt to connect, we need to tell them that the game is full; we'll do this through an error message. And if the game is ready to begin, we'll start the game. Here's the code for addPlayer, sendGameFullMessage, and startGame (which calls resetGame, which we'll write soon):

```
const addPlayer = (stanza) => {
  if (playerJids.length <2) {
    playerJids.push(stanza.jid)
    sendDimensions(
        playerJids[numPlayers],
        {
            width,
            height,
            paddleWidth,
            paddleHeight,
            paddleMargin,
            paddleY,
            ballRadius,
            side: playerJids.length
        }
    )
    score.push(0)
    if (playerJids.length === 2) startGame()
  } else if (playerJids.length >= 2) {
    sendGameFullMessage(stanza.attrs.from)
  }
}

const sendGameFullMessage = (to) => {
  const errorStanza = new ltx.Element('message', { type: 'error', to })
    .c('error', { type: 'cancel' })
    .c('conflict', { xmlns: 'urn:ietf:params:xml:ns:xmpp-stanzas' })
    .c('text')
```

```
        .t('Game is currently full')
        component.send(errorStanza)
}

const startGame = () => {
    gameState = 1
    resetGame()
}
```

Now that we have written the code for players to join the game, let's set up the game loop.

# Setting up a game loop in the component

We will need to add a game loop to the component to keep the game in motion. The component will respond to incoming messages that will affect the status of the game (e.g., the position of paddles in the game). We need to make sure the component can take some actions on its own (e.g., moving the ball), so we need a way to make actions happen without waiting for incoming messages – hence, the need for the game loop.

We could create our own game loop logic, but fortunately there is an existing open source game loop designed for Node servers. It's called node-gameloop, and you can find it at: https://www.npmjs.com/package/node-gameloop. This package is simple to use. It has two API methods: setGameLoop, which creates a game loop, and clearGameLoop, which stops a game loop. The actions that should take place during each step in the loop, and the time that should pass between each step in the game loop (measured in milliseconds) are passed as a function to setGameLoop.

To install node-gameloop enter the following:

```
npm install node-gameloop
```

Now we can make the following adjustments to the server code:

1. At the very beginning of the index.js file that we just created, you'll notice that we already have the following line:

   ```
   const Gameloop = require("node-gameloop");
   ```

2. Add the following function at the end of the index.js:

   ```
   const id = Gameloop.setGameLoop(updateGame, 1000 / 30) /* 30 fps */
   ```

Notice our new call to updateGame(). This is a function that we will write to contain the code that moves the ball as the game is played.

Now that we have a game loop in the component, the component can start managing aspects of the game on its own.

## Starting and updating the game

Now it's time for our `startGame()` and `updateGame()` functions. `startGame()` is going to be really simple: it will just set the `gameState` variable to *1* to show that the game is running. This is called when the second player joins the game:

```
const startGame = () => {
    gameState = 1
    resetGame()
}
```

Of course, `updateGame()` is more interesting. That function will move the ball, check to see if the ball hits or misses anything (in particular, paddles and the top and bottom walls), and update the players with ball position updates and score updates, if one player happens to sneak the ball past the other's paddle.

Let's start with this first part of the function, which will leave the `updateGame()` function if the game is not in progress:

```
const updateGame = () => {
    if (gameState !== 1) return
```

## Maintaining the ball state in the component

As we discussed earlier, the server-side component will maintain the position and direction of the ball. Let's start by bringing in some variables related to the ball that we previously saw in the clients.

Recall that we have these variables to work with:

```
let ballX, ballY
const ballRadius = 3
let ballHeading; // degrees
let ballSpeed;  // pixels per millisecond
```

In the version of the code from the last chapter, we maintained two variables, `ballDeltaX` and `ballDeltaY`, to indicate the direction of the ball. In this version, we are going to do something slightly different. We will maintain the ball's heading, in radians (with 0 meaning straight to the right and increasing counter-clockwise; a full circle contains `2*PI radians`), and the ball's speed. This means that we will need a little basic trigonometry to figure out the ball's updated location when the game loop is run. One reason we did not do this in the client version is that we would have had to have trigonometry code in multiple places. This would have been a bit too much detail in the client-only version, but with our server-side component, we're getting a bit more serious.

If you are not familiar with the sine and cosine functions in trigonometry, or if you need a quick refresher, this next paragraph is for you.

Imagine we have a ball at position (*a, b*) heading in direction *d*, and we know that the distance the ball will travel in direction *d* is the ball's speed (in pixels/milliseconds) over a duration of milliseconds. For example, a ball at position (1, 1) moving at PI radians at a speed of 20 pixels/milliseconds over 10 milliseconds. Simple math tells us that the total distance that the ball will travel is 200 pixels. Now, we need to figure out how many pixels in the X direction, and how many pixels in the Y direction, the ball will actually move. Let's call those distances `deltaX` and `deltaY`. We can imagine a triangle of `deltaX`, `deltaY`, and 200 as the hypotenuse. Now here's where sine and cosine come in. The length of the hypotenuse multiplied by the sine of the angle will give us `deltaX`, and the length of the hypotenuse multiplied by the cosine of the angle will give us `deltaY`. (The way I've remembered this for years is by using two made-up words, `sinx` and `cosy`, which tell me *sine is for x* and *cosine is for y*) Our ball, therefore, has a `deltaX` of `200*sin(pi)` and `deltaY` of `200*cos(pi)`.

Remember, these are deltas, so we need to add these values to the original position. And don't worry about needing to figure out if you add or subtract the deltas from the original position. The sine and cosine functions will return negative values (sine returns negative values for parameters greater than pi and less than `2*pi`, and cosine returns negative values for parameters greater than pi/2 and less than `3*pi/2`), so you can add any resulting value to the x and y components of the original position to get an accurate updated position.

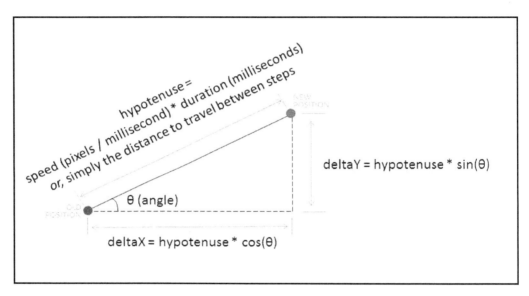

Thus ends our math lesson. All of this talk really boils down to these next two lines, which you can add to the updateGame() function (and, we're simplifying a bit by not maintaining a delta-time and multiplying the speed by it to get a distance):

```
//Update the ball's position
ballX = ballX + Math.cos(ballHeading) * ballSpeed
ballY = ballY + Math.sin(ballHeading) * ballSpeed
```

Of course, we don't want the server to update the ball position without telling the clients! Let's make sure to pass the message along. Actually, we'll write this function later, but let's at least call it here:

```
sendBallPosition(ballX, ballY)
```

As per the table of messages we introduced earlier, let's keep in mind that our clients will need to listen for this message and update their displays according.

# Bounces and misses

There is more that we will need to do for the ball position. For example, we will need to check whether the ball has bounced off a paddle, or whether it has left the field of play.

Fortunately, we have already established the dimensions of the playing field. Here is what we need to watch for within the component:

- If the ball's new position hits one of the player's paddles, bounce the ball back into the playfield
- If the ball's new position touches (or is slightly beyond) the top or bottom edges of the playing field, bounce the ball back into the playfield
- If the ball's new position is to the left or right of the established playfield, one of the players has missed the ball and the other player has just scored a point

In the first two cases, bounce the ball back into the playing field means calculating a new heading for the ball. If you want, you can also have a little fun with adjusting the ball's heading and speed depending on where on the paddle the ball was hit. For example, if the ball hits the paddle toward the top or bottom ends of the paddle, perhaps the ball ricochets off at a wider angle than if it were to hit the paddle squarely in the middle. Since our focus is on XMPP messaging rather than the advanced physics of Pong, we'll leave that as an exercise for the reader.

Here is the code:

```
    // Check if the ball has hit the left paddle
  if (
      ((ballX - ballRadius) <= playfieldMinX + paddleMargin +
      paddleWidth) && (ballY + ballRadius > paddleY[0]) &&
      (ballY - ballRadius < paddleY[0] + paddleHeight[0])
  ) {
    if ((ballHeading > Math.PI / 2.0) && (ballHeading <= Math.PI)) {
      ballHeading = Math.PI - ballHeading
    }
    if ((ballHeading > Math.PI) && (ballHeading <= 3.0 * Math.PI / 2.0))
    {
      ballHeading = 3.0 * Math.PI - ballHeading
    }
  }
  // Check if the ball has hit the right paddle
```

```
if (
    (ballX + ballRadius >= playfieldMaxX - paddleMargin - paddleWidth)
      && (ballY + ballRadius > paddleY[1]) &&
    (ballY - ballRadius < paddleY[1] + paddleHeight[1])
) {
    if ((ballHeading > 3.0 * Math.PI / 2.0) && (ballHeading <=
      2.0 * Math.PI))
    {
        ballHeading = 3.0*Math.PI - ballHeading
    }
    if ((ballHeading > 0) && (ballHeading < Math.PI / 2.0)) {
        ballHeading = Math.PI - ballHeading
    }
}
// Check if ball has hit the top of the playfied
if (ballY - ballRadius <= playfieldMinY) {
    ballHeading = 2.0 * Math.PI - ballHeading
}
// Check if ball has hit the bottom of the playfield
if (ballY + ballRadius >= playfieldMaxY) {
    ballHeading = 2.0 * Math.PI - ballHeading
}
// Check if the ball has been missed by the left player
if (ballX - ballRadius <= playfieldMinX) {
    updateScore(+0, +1)
    resetGame()
}
// Check if the ball has been missed by the right player
if (ballX + ballRadius >= playfieldMaxX) {
    updateScore(+1, +0)
    resetGame()
}
```

At this point, we have updated the ball position and checked for whether the ball is bouncing off the top and bottom walls or colliding with the paddles (or missing the paddles, resulting in a point for one of the players). There is only one thing left to do: recognize when the game should end and close up updateGame():

```
        if ((score[0] === 10) || (score[1] === 10)) {
            endGame()
        }
    }
}
```

When the ball misses one of the paddles, we'll need to reset the game, which can be done using resetGame() function (remember, we also call this from the startGame() function):

```
const resetGame = () => {
```

```
    ballX = playfieldWidth / 2.0
    ballY = playfieldHeight / 2.0
    ballHeading = Math.random() * 2.0 * Math.PI
    ballSpeed = 2
    sendBallPosition({ x : ballX, y : ballY })
}
```

When the maximum score of 10 has been reached by either player, we'll need to end the game. We'll also use this as a chance for the component to clear the array of current players, so players at other browsers can have their turn at playing. The endGame() function is just as simple as startGame():

```
const endGame = () => {
    gameState = 2
    playerJids = []
    sendGameOver()
}
```

Let's not forget that there is a score that needs to be updated! The updateScore method will take two values: The amount to add to Player 1's score, and the amount to add to Player 2's score. Since these are amounts to add rather than absolute amounts, I prefer to use an explicit plus character next to the parameter, as you saw above (for example, updateScore(+1, +0);). I think this helps communicate that the score is increasing by 1 (or increasing by 0, whatever that means, although it feels okay to me) rather than being set to 1 and 0. (By the way, you can use the same method to decrease a player's score... which might be something you want to do if you implement some kind of power-up in this game!)

```
const updateScore = (player1delta, player2delta) => {
    score[0] += player1delta
    score[1] += player2delta
    sendScoreUpdate({ player1 : score[0], player2 : score[1] })
}
```

# Expecting paddle updates

Just as the server will update the ball position and send updates to the clients, the clients will be responsible for passing along updates to the paddle positions for their respective players. The server will need to listen to those paddle updates, and those will be handled by incoming messages rather than by the game loop.

On the server side, we are already expecting to handle the paddle position message, so let's fill that in. The paddle update will need to receive two pieces of data: The ID of the client moving the paddle, and the new paddle position.

We also need to remember that when one client sends a paddle update, the second client needs to know about it! In addition to updating the paddle location with respect to the server, we will also need to pass this information along to the opponent's client:

```
const receivePaddlePosition = (playerSide, paddleY) => {
    paddleY[playerSide] = paddleY
    sendOpponentPaddlePosition( { y : paddleY })
}
```

Finally, the last function in your component at this point should be the game loop code we added earlier.

There are our core game control methods. Now let's see how to implement the messages being sent to and from the component.

# Implementing messages from the component to the clients

Let's take a look at the code we just wrote particularly updateGame() and updatePaddlePosition(), but don't forget addPlayer() and see what messages we promised to send to the clients. Here again is the list, derived from the table at the beginning of this chapter:

- sendDimensions: Sent to the player who was just added
- sendBallPosition: Sent to both players
- sendScoreUpdate: Sent to both players
- sendOpponentPaddlePosition: Sent to the player receiving the other's update
- sendGameOver: Sent to both players

Not too long of a list. Let's implement these messages. Keep in mind that we will be using a payload that we define specifically for XMPPong in these messages. We will essentially use ltx to construct the message stanza, then send it to the clients using component.send(stanza).

Here is the implementation of the messages:

```
const sendDimensions = (dimensions) => {
    const stanza = new ltx.Element('message', { to: componentJid })
    stanza.c('body').t('dimensions')
    const pong = stanza.c('pong', { xmlns: PONG_NAMESPACE })
    for (let key in dimensions) {
```

```
            pong.c(key).t(dimensions[key])
        }
        pong.c('action').t('dimensions')
        component.send(stanza)
}
const sendBallPosition = (position) => {
        const stanza = new ltx.Element('message', { from: componentJid })
        stanza.c('body').t('ballposition')
        const pong = stanza.c('pong', { xmlns: PONG_NAMESPACE }).c('position')
        pong.c('x').t(position.x)
        pong.c('y').t(position.y)
        pong.c('action').t('ballPosition')
        playerJids.forEach((playerJid) => {
            stanza.attrs.to = playerJid
            component.send(stanza)
        })
}
const sendScoreUpdate = (score) => {
        const stanza = new ltx.Element('message', { from: componentJid })
        stanza.c('body').t('scoreUpdate')
        const pong = stanza.c('pong', { xmlns: PONG_NAMESPACE })
        pong.c('score').t(score)
        pong.c('action').t('scoreUpdate')
        playerJids.forEach((playerJid) => {
            stanza.attrs.to = playerJid
            component.send(stanza)
        })
}
const sendOpponentPaddlePosition = (y) => {
        const stanza = new ltx.Element('message', { from: componentJid })
        stanza.c('body').t('opponentpaddleupdate')
        cosnt pong stanza.c('pong', { xmlns: PONG_NAMESPACE })
        pong.c('y').t(y)
        pong.c('action').t('opponentPaddleUpdate')
        playerJids.forEach((playerJid) => {
            stanza.attrs.to = playerJid
            component.send(stanza)
        })
}
const sendGameOver = () => {
        const stanza = new ltx.Element('message', { from: componentJid })
        stanza.c('body').t('gameOver')
        stanza.c('pong', { xmlns: PONG_NAMESPACE })
        .c('action').t('gameOver')
        playerJids.forEach((playerJid) => {
            stanza.attrs.to = playerJid
            component.send(stanza)
        })
```

```
}
```

# Handling incoming messages from the clients

So far, we have written the code necessary to send messages from the component to the clients. Remember that we also have two messages that we are expecting from the clients:

- `playerCheckingIn`: Sent from a client when the client wishes to join the game
- `paddlePosition`: Sent from a client when the player has moved their paddle

To handle incoming messages, we need to tell the component how to respond to incoming stanzas. The best place for the following code is near the top of your `index.js` file, just below the variable declarations:

```
component.on('stanza', (stanza) => {
    if (true === stanza.is('iq')) {
        handleIq(stanza)
    } else if (true === stanza.is('message')) {
        handleMessage(stanza)
    }
})
```

It's the `handleMessage()` function, that will be triggered when we get one of the game messages we're expecting. As we write `handleMessage()`, we want to keep a couple of things in mind. First, we want to ensure that we're actually getting an XMPPong message. Second, we want to ensure that the message is indeed from our opponent, and not from some other client attempting to throw our game off! Here is the code for `handleMessage()`:

```
const handleMessage = (stanza) => {
    const pong = stanza.getChild('pong', PONG_NAMESPACE)
    if (!pong) return
    const action = pong.getChildText('action')
    /* Is message from one of the players? If no, ignore? or add to game?
*/
    if (-1 !== playerJids.indexOf(stanza.attrs.from)) {
      console.log("Received message from someone besides our expected
opponent!")
      return
    }
    /* Switch on 'body' and perform required action */
    if (action === 'playercheckingin') {
      addPlayer(stanza)
    } else if (action === 'paddleposition') {
```

```
    receivePaddlePosition(stanza.attrs.pong.getChildText(y))
    }
  }
```

We see the call to addPlayer(), which we have already introduced. We also see a new call to receivePaddlePosition(), which we have not yet written. Let's implement that:

```
const receivePaddlePosition = (playerSide, paddleY) => {
    paddleY[playerSide] = paddleY
    sendOpponentPaddlePosition(playerSide,  { y : paddleY } )
}
```

We now have an XMPPong component that can send and receive messages! There is one other message that we want to handle before we move on to other portions of the project, and that's the IQ message.

# Handing DISCO#info requests

The one last bit that we want to complete is the handleIq() function that we alluded to in the handleMessage() function. This function will respond with a message giving the capabilities offered by this server-side component specifically, its ability to play XMPPong, which is indicated in part by the identity of the reply as well as the feature that contains the XMPPong namespace:

```
const handleIq = (stanza) => {
    const query = stanza.getChild('query',
       'http://jabber.org/protocol/disco#info')
    if (!query) return
    const reply = new Stanza(
      'iq',
      {
        type: 'result',
    id: stanza.attrs.id,
    from: stanza.attrs.to,
    to: stanza.attrs.from
      }
    )
     .c('query', { xmlns: 'http://jabber.org/protocol/disco#info' })
     reply.c('identity',{category: 'chat', name: 'XMPPong', type:'text'})
     reply.c('feature', { var: PONG_NAMESPACE })
     component.send(reply)
     console.log(`Replied to DISCO#info with ${reply.root().toString()}`)
}
```

And now, we're ready to move on to the XMPP-FTW extension to work with messages in our own custom format.

# Creating an XMPP-FTW extension to read messages within our namespace

The XMPP-FTW extension allows us to develop a server and build stanzas that use our own custom message format.

The concept is simple: A list of events at the beginning of the script specify which functions should be called when a certain event is received from the browser. The functions build the appropriate stanza before sending it out via the XMPP client connection (and on to our component via the XMPP server). You can see one of the most basic extensions, one for ping messages, here at https://github.com/xmpp-ftw/xmpp-ftw-ping.

Let's understand more about how this works. XMPP-FTW acts as an XMPP client and has a websocket connection to the browser. The browser emits events with an event name, a payload, and maybe a callback function. XMPP-FTW then converts this payload into an XML stanza and sends it through the client connection to the XMPP server.

The XMPP server sends XML to the client, which XMPP-FTW picks up via the handles() and handle() functions – handles() returns a Boolean indicating whether the XML can be handled, and handle() does the work of actually managing the XML. The handle() function translates the XML into a payload and the appropriate event name, then emits this back to the browser.

Let's build one of these for XMPPong. To start, Recall that we defined the XML content of the messages in the table earlier in this chapter. Keeping this in mind will help us craft the extension.

Create a file called pong-extension.js, and let's start populating it with some imports and a constructor:

```
'use strict';
const ltx  = require('ltx')
    , Base = require('xmpp-ftw').Base
var PongExt = function() {}
PongExt.prototype = new Base()
```

We also want to define the XMPPong namespace, so add the following declaration:

```
PongExt.prototype.NS_PONG = 'urn:xmpp:game:pong'
```

Next, we want to indicate the messages that the extension can expect to receive from the browser to pass along to the server. As you'll recall, those are the `playerCheckingIn` and `paddlePosition` messages. When these messages are identified, we want to call a function to deal with those messages. Provide values to the prototype `variable` `_events` like this:

```
PongExt.prototype._events = {
    playercheckingin: 'receivePlayerCheckingIn',
    paddleposition: 'receivePaddlePosition'
}
```

Let's implement those receive functions. In each, we will be receiving data from a message from the browser (you'll see that when we create the client code), and we will take data from these messages to form the stanza that we'll send to the server.

```
PongExt.prototype.receivePlayerCheckingIn = function(data) {
    /*
       Direction: Browser to server
       Event: 'playercheckingin'
       Payload: { to: $componentJid, position: $yPosition }
    */
    const stanza = new ltx.Element('message', { to: data.to })
    stanza.c('body').t('playercheckingin')
    stanza.c('pong', { xmlns: this.NS_PONG
}).c('action').t('playercheckingin')
    this.manager.client.send(stanza)
}
PongExt.prototype.receivePaddlePosition = function(data) {
    /*
       Direction: Browser to server
       Event: 'playercheckingin'
       Payload: { to: $componentJid, position: $yPosition }
    */
    const stanza = new ltx.Element('message', { to: data.to })
      stanza.c('body').t('paddleposition')
    const pong = stanza.c('pong', { xmlns: this.NS_PONG })
    pong.c('action').t('paddleposition')
    pong.c('y').t(data.position)
    this.manager.client.send(stanza)
}
```

Recall that the extension also lets us implement handles() to know whether the extension can handle a certain type of message from the server to the client, and handle() to actually emit that message on the socket.

Here is our handles() function, which replies true if the stanza passed to the function uses the XMPPong namespace:

```
PongExt.prototype.handles = function(stanza) {
    if (!stanza.is('message')) return false
    const pong = stanza.getChild('pong', this.NS_PONG)
    if (pong) {
        return true
    } else {
        return false
    }
}
```

And here is the handle() function. Actually, we'll delegate to the _handleMessage() function, and within that message we'll generate a data payload based on the information from the given stanza:

```
PongExt.prototype.handle = function(stanza) {
    if (stanza.is('message')) {
        this._handleMessage(stanza)
    }
}
/* Event names here equal the text of the <action/> element
   Payloads (to the browser) are what you see in the 'data'
   variable, not JID is parsed into parts (local, domain, resource)
   for the component just 'domain' would be populated
 */
PongExt.prototype._handleMessage = function(stanza) {
    const pong = stanza.getChild('pong')
    const action = pong.getChildText('action')
    let data = null
    switch (action) {
        case 'scoreupdate':
            const player1 = pong.getChildText('player1')
            const player2 = pong.getChildText('player2')
            data = { player1, player2 }
            break
        case 'dimensions':
            const data = {}
            pong.children.forEach((child) => {
              data[child.getName()] = child.getText()
            })
            break
```

```
        case 'ballposition':
            const data = {
                x: pong.getChildText('x'),
                y: pong.getChildText('y')
            }
            break
        case 'opponentpaddleupdate':
            const data = {
                y: pong.getChildText('y')
            }
            break
        case 'gameover':
            data = {}
            break
    }
    if (data) {
        data.from = this._getJid(stanza.attrs.from)
        this.socket.send(action, data)
    }
}
```

You're pretty much done with the XMPP-FTW extension at this point. Just make sure to export the module at the end of the code:

```
module.exports = PongExt
```

One more thing before we move on: We need to call this extension from the XMPP-FTW Skeleton. Recall there is an index.js in the ~/pong folder. We will need to edit that file and insert our extension.

At the beginning of the file, include the following line with the imports:

```
const PongExtension = require('/path/to/pong-extension')
```

And, in the primus.on() function, you'll need to add the XMPPong extension as a listener:

```
xmppFtw.addListener(new PongExtension())
```

Now you're good to go with the extension! On to the third part of our project: the client!

# Developing the client

One of the cool things about having a server with a known set of expected messages is that the clients can look like anything you can imagine, as long as they send and respond to the expected set of messages. Not every client needs to look alike nor have the same output – for example, there's no reason we couldn't have one of our XMPPong players gaming from a terminal window! We will keep our client basic, since we want to demonstrate the use of XMPP rather than get crazy with HTML and CSS, but you are welcome to be as creative as you'd like here. In fact, you could toss in some D3 or even create a client using Unity or any other framework, as long as you can send and receive those XMPP messages.

Recall from the table earlier in this chapter that we need our browser (in this case) to connect to the XMPP-FTW server and expect, or send, the following events:

- Send a request to the client  wishes to connect to a game (outgoing: `playercheckingin`)
- Listen for default dimensions, like playing field size (incoming: `dimensions`)
- Listen for ball updates (incoming: `ballposition`)
- Send paddle updates (outgoing: `paddleposition`)
- Listen for updates to the opponent's paddle (incoming: `opponentpaddleupdate`)
- Listen for score updates (incoming: `scoreupdate` )
- Listen for game over messages (incoming: `gameover`)

Let's get started!

# Starting the XMPP-FTW server

To write the XMPP-FTW server, we will want to use the XMPP-FTW skeleton. Rather than start from scratch, we will commandeer the client code we already started in the previous chapter since we have already done so much work on drawing on the HTML canvas. This will lighten our load in this chapter and let us focus on passing the messages.

Before we get started, let's make a copy of the original Pong client we created in Chapter 8, *Building a Basic XMPP-Based Pong Game* and set it aside:

```
cd ~/pong/public/scripts
cp pong.js pong_chapter8.js
```

And let's do the same with `index.ejs` in the views folder:

```
cd ~/pong/views
cp index.ejs index_chapter8.ejs
```

Now we'll edit the `pong.js` and `index.ejs` files, keeping the `_chapter8` files untouched in case you would like to go back and revisit those (Note: If you do want to revisit the work you did for Chapter 8, *Building a Basic XMPP-Based Pong Game* you will need to update `index_chapter8.ejs` to point to `pong_chapter8.js`).

Let's start making some changes to `pong.ejs` to match our new component. First, replace the Global variables and the Player variables near the beginning of the code with the following:

```
// Global variables
let width, height
let paddleMargin
let paddleWidth
let ballRadius
// Player variables
let paddleMargin, paddleWidth
let paddleHeight[], paddle[]
let ballRadius
let ballX, ballY
let side
let player1score, player2score
let gameOver = false
```

Keep the `mouseDown`, canvas, and context variables. In other words, keep this block:

```
var mouseDown = false
var canvas = document.getElementById('pong')
var context = canvas.getContext('2d')
```

Let's make sure our socket code persists as well, and that the `connect()` function gets us a connection:

```
    var socket = new Primus('//' + window.document.location.host)
socket.on('error'), function(error) { console.error(error) }
    socket.on('timeout', function(reason) {
        console.error('Connection failed: ' + reason)
    })
    socket.on('end', function() {
        console.log('Socket connection closed')
        socket = null
    })
    socket.on('xmpp.error', function(error) {
```

```
        console.error('XMPP-FTW error', error)
})
socket.on('xmpp.error.client', function(error) {
        console.error('XMPP-FTW client error', error)
})
socket.on('xmpp.chat.message', handleMessage)
socket.on('xmpp.discover.client', handleDisco)

function connect()  {
    var Client = require('node-xmpp-client')
    var options = {
        jid: document.getElementById('username').value,
        password: document.getElementById('password').value
    }
    var client = new Client(options)
    client.on('stanza', handleMessage(stanza))
    client.once('online', function(connectionDetails) {
        console.log(options.jid+' is connected!')
        console.log(connectionDetails)
    })
}
```

In `init()`, remove the call to `resetBallLocationAndDelta` and, in fact, remove that function from the code. The clients will no longer set the ball location, that is now done by the component, and the clients will listen for updates to the ball position. While you're removing `resetBallLocationAndDelta`, also remove `updateBallPosition` for the same reason. And since the component is managing our game loop, we can get rid of the game loop function from the client.

We'll also need to let the component know we're checking in, so we'll create a message for that and send it.

Here's the new `init()`:

```
function init() {
 // Prevent I-Beam cursor from appearing on mousedown
canvas.onselectstart = function () { return false }
 canvas.addEventListener('mousedown', doMouseDownEvent, false)
 canvas.addEventListener('mouseup', doMouseUpEvent, false)
 canvas.addEventListener('mousemove', doMouseMoveEvent, false)
 // We'll be putting a check-in message here shortly!
}
```

While we're keeping functions, let's make sure to maintain the mouse event functions:

```
function doMouseDownEvent(event) {
  mouseDown = true
  setPad1Position(event.layerY)
}
function doMouseUpEvent(event) {
  mouseDown = false
}
function doMouseMoveEvent(event) {
  if (mouseDown) {
    setPad1Position(event.layerY)
  }
}
```

Now we're ready for the fun parts: Sending and Receiving XMPP messages!

# Checking in to the component and receiving dimensions

Remember that one of the first messages the client needs to send is a check-in to the component. When the component receives this message, it will assign the first client the left side of the playfield, and the second client the right side of the playfield. When the client checks in with the component, this also triggers the component to send the client a set of dimensions that the client can use to draw an appropriately-sized playfield.

In the `init()` method, add a call to send the checking in message:

```
// Send check-in message
socket.send('playercheckingin', { to:
document.getElementById('componentJid').value })
```

We have several messages that we're expecting. Specifically, if we recall the tables from this chapter, the client is awaiting these messages from the component:

- Dimensions
- Updates to the ball position
- Updates to the opponent's paddle position
- Updates to the score
- A Game Over message

We'll want to use `socket.on()` to look for these messages, passing functions that can process the incoming data. For example, we will want to look for the dimensions message, and when it comes in, we'll call a function called `handleDimensionsMessage()`.

Here are the `socket.on()` listeners that we want to set up:

```
socket.on('dimensions', handleDimensionMessage)
socket.on('gameOver', handleGameOverMessage)
socket.on('ballPosition', handleBallPositionMessage)
socket.on('opponentPaddleUpdate', handleOpponentPaddleUpdateMessage)
socket.on('updateScore', handleUpdateScoreMessage)
```

Now on to writing each of those delegate messages. The Dimensions messagee will be the longest, because there are many variables to parse from it. In each case, we just need to dig into the stanza and pull out the values that are important:

```
function handleDimensionMessage(data) {
    width = data.width
    height = data.height
    paddleWidth = data.paddlewidth
    paddleHeight[0] = data.paddleheight
    paddleHeight[1] = data.paddleheight
    paddleMargin = data.paddlemargin
    paddle[0] = data.paddley
    paddle[1] = data.paddley
    ballRadius = data.ballradius
    side = data.side
}
```

 By the way, if you've been wondering why we're maintaining an array of paddle heights, this is to encourage you (or challenge you, or invite you) to implement a capability in which the player who just scored a point finds their paddle shortened a little so the next point is not won so easily. You'll have to create a new message to convey this information and update the paddle height.

Handling the ball position is easy:

```
function handleBallPositionMessage(data) {
  ballX = data.x
  ballY = data.y
}
```

And the opponent's paddle update:

```
function handleOpponentPaddleUpdateMessage(data) {
    paddle[1-side] = data.y
}
```

And the score update:

```
function handleUpdateScoreMessage(data) {
    player1score = data.player1score
    player2score = data.player2score
}
```

And, finally, the Game Over message:

```
function handleGameOverMessage(data) {
  gameOver = true
}
```

Phew, that's a lot of stuff! But look at what we've done: We have pretty much implemented all of the message handling that we need at this point!

We do have one outstanding message. Remember that we need to send updates to the component when the player moves their paddle. We need a sendPaddleUpdate message, and here it is:

```
function sendPaddleUpdate() {
    socket.send('paddleposition', { to: componentJid, y: paddle[side]
})
    console.log('Sent new paddle position = ', paddle[side])
}
```

We're almost ready to play XMPPong! Let's just make sure we have the right drawing code in place in the client.

# Drawing code in the client

If you've started from your Chapter 8, *Building a Basic XMPP-Based Pong Game* code, you already have these functions in place, but in case you need them again, or if you just want to make sure you have the right code in place, here are the drawing functions that will complete the client:

```
function clearField() {
  context.fillStyle = "#FFFFFF"
  context.fillRect(0, 0, width, height)
  context.strokeStyle = "#000000"
  context.strokeRect(0, 0, width, height)
}
function drawBall() {
  context.beginPath()
  context.arc(ballX, ballY, ballRadius, 0, Math.PI * 2, false)
  context.fillStyle = "#C11B17"
  context.fill()
  context.strokeStyle = "#9F000F"
  context.stroke()
}
function drawPaddle(x, y, w, h) {
  context.fillStyle = "#306EFF"
  context.fillRect(x, y, w, h)
  context.strokeStyle = "#2B65EC"
  context.strokeRect(x, y, w, h)
}

function drawPaddles() {
  drawPaddle(paddleMargin, paddle[0], paddleWidth, paddleHeight[0])
  drawPaddle(width - paddleMargin - paddleWidth, paddle[1], paddleWidth,
paddleHeight[1])
}

function drawScore() {
  context.font = "36px Arial"
  context.fillStyle = "#000000"
  context.fillText(player1score, width / 2 - 100 -
  context.measureText(player1score).width, 40)
  context.fillText(player2score, width / 2 + 100, 40)
}
```

We also had one function to set the paddle position. This function makes sure that the paddle position is valid before sending the appropriate message. This is called from doMouseMoveEvent().

```
function setPaddlePosition(candidateY) {
  if ((candidateY > 0) && (candidateY < height)) {
    paddle[side] = candidateY
    sendPaddleUpdate(paddle[side])
  }
}
```

Finally, make sure you have a few other socket.on functions defined:

```
socket.on('open', function() {
  console.log('Connected')
})
socket.on('timeout', function(reason) {
  console.error('Connection failed: ' + reason)
})
socket.on('end', function() {
  console.log('Socket connection closed')
  socket = null
})

socket.on('xmpp.error', function(error) {
  console.error('XMPP-FTW error', error)
})
socket.on('xmpp.error.client', function(error) {
  console.error('XMPP-FTW client error', error)
})
```

Close out your code with a final }), and we're good to go!

# Modifying the browser view

One last thing we need to do is go to the index.ejs file and change some things there. Using the same index.ejs as from the previous chapter, we're going to change the opponent field with a field that will let us indicate which server we wish to connect to – in other words, the component JID of the XMPPong game.

The way this would work in reality is that a client would use DISCO to discover the capabilities of the server. If the response indicated that there was an XMPPong capability available on the server, this would be made available to the client – provided that the client understands how to play Pong, of course!

In index.ejs, simply change the phrase Opponent JID to Component JID, and change the id of opponent to componentJid.

# Running the server and clients

At this point, you have a functioning server-side component and functioning clients, so it's time to see them working together, sending messages back and forth, and letting you get a good game of Pong in before lunchtime. Ready?

Your server component may already be running. If not, restart the Prosody service using the following command:

```
sudo service prosody start
```

Run the component from the pong-component directory:

```
node index.js
```

For the clients, open a second terminal window, navigate to the directory with the client's index.js code and run that (node index.js), then open a browser and visit http://localhost:3000.

You may want to open a second browser, also point it to http://localhost:3000, and get your own one-on-one Pong game going.

# Summary

In this chapter, you have built a complete application with a server-side component, an XMPP-FTW extension for adding messages with your own namespace, and clients that connect to the server and send messages back and forth. Hopefully you've had some fun while gaining deeper knowledge that demonstrates how you can apply XMPP in your own real-world applications.

Speaking about real-world applications, when you do develop your business applications and consider deploying them, there are several factors that you'll need to keep in mind regarding concerns of security, scalability, and so on. Fortunately, XMPP provides powerful capabilities to support your deployed, real-world applications, and you're going to learn about those in the next chapter.

You will also read more about various XMPP Extension Protocols (XEPs), and get a sense for how XMPP continues to grow in a world that is evolving toward new things like Universal Plug and Play, the Internet of Things, and WebRTC.

# 10
# Real-World Deployment and XMPP Extensions

XMPP servers are capable of more than sending messages between clients and servers or server components. When you are building a real-world XMPP-based application, you will need to ensure that your application has adequate security and that your application can scale to support growing needs. You may need to ensure that the server side of your application works in an ecosystem with other services.

In Chapter 1, *An Introduction to XMPP and Installing Our First Server* we introduced the use of Prosody as our XMPP server. In this chapter, we will continue to use Prosody to explore these features. Other servers (for example, Openfire, Tigase, MongooseIM, and ejabberd) also support these features. If you need to know which servers provide which features, Wikipedia has such a page: https://en.wikipedia.org/wiki/Comparison_of_XMPP_serv er_software. Often, you can find a list of extensions that each server supports; for example, the protocols that Openfire supports can be found at: http://download.igniterealtime.o rg/openfire/docs/latest/documentation/protocol-support.html.

The features we are about to discuss are all described in XMPP Extension Protocols, or XEPs (pronounced "**zeps**"). Later in this chapter, we will talk more about the XMPP Standards Foundation (XSF) and the development of XEPs to support new features. We will also take a look at several up-and-coming extensions that are guaranteed to propel XMPP into the future. But for our first step, we will look at ways we can extend the capabilities of our server.

# Server Modules

Whether you use Prosody, Tigase, ejabberd, or the XMPP server of your choice, you will have the ability to install server modules, components that extend the capabilities of your server and that can be independently installed, enabled or disabled, and configured. Some modules might provide capabilities to support a XEP, some might provide integration with databases and other storage frameworks, and so on. At the time of writing, Prosody has 230 modules, which you can explore at `https://modules.prosody.im`. Together, these modules comprise the prosody-modules project. The source code for these modules is located on Prosody's Mercurial site, `https://hg.prosody.im/prosody-modules`, and you can pull them down easily using Mercurial.

If you do not yet have Mercurial, you can apply the following steps:

```
$ sudo apt-get install mercurial
$ mkdir ~/prosody-modules
$ cd prosody-modules
$ hg clone https://hg.prosody.im/prosody-modules
```

When, at some point, you want to update the files in your clone enter the following:

```
$ cd ~/prosody-modules and $ hg pull --update
```

Your Prosody server has a standard folder where it expects to find plugins (for example, `/usr/lib/prosody/modules`, or what `prosodyctl about` lists for the plugin directory), but Prosody can also look in more than one location for plugins; these locations are set in the `plugin_paths` variable in your configuration file, `prosody.cfg.lua`; `prosody_paths` is an array of paths to search for plugins, and they are searched in the order that the paths appear in the array.

Let's bring one of these modules into the server so you can see how to do this, since we'll be using modules in a couple of sections in this chapter. The module we will install in this example is called `mod_webpresence`, and it lets you include an image on your website that reflects your XMPP status on the server. You can find it at: `https://modules.prosody.im/mod_webpresence.html`.

This module happens to be easy to install. You'll need to place a copy of the `mod_webpresence.lua` file into Prosody's modules folder, `/usr/lib/prosody/modules` (or, if not there, you can use `prosodyctl about`, which will show the plugin directory). Copy it from `~/prosody-modules/mod_webpresence`. While there is also an icons folder there, the icons are also represented in the Lua file itself, so you will not need to copy the icon images. Copy the Lua file to your plugin directory (remember, `/usr/lib/prosody/modules`, or what `prosodyctl about` tells you):

```
$ cd ~/prosody-modules/mod_webpresence
$ sudo cp mod_webpresence.lua /usr/lib/prosody/modules
```

Now we need to let Prosody know that we have a new module that we would like to have the server use. Open your configuration file, `prosody.cfg.lua`, and add `webpresence` to the list of `modules_enabled`. (Note that is no `mod_` in that string.)

Save, exit, stop, and start Prosody, and your module will take effect!

You can test this module simply by creating a quick HTML page that shows the status of the `test@localhost` account we created earlier. Create a file called `webpresence-test.html` with the following content:

```
<!DOCTYPE html>
<title>mod_webpresence test</title>
<img src="http://localhost:5280/status/test" />
```

Load the HTML file in a browser of your choice; you should see a status for the `test@localhost` account.

Enjoy exploring the many Prosody modules. Be sure to pay attention to their implementation status. While many are ready for real-world use, some are proofs of concept, and some others are just for fun.

# DNS setup and SRV records

Suppose you have a number of services that you want to make available, and you would like each service to have a unique Domain Name System (DNS) entry. To do this, you could establish service records (also known as SRV records) for those services. An SRV record lets you associate the name of a service with the server that provides the service. You may want to set this up for your XMPP services (provided you have a domain name associated with your XMPP server).

An SRV record has the following format, each element separated by a single space:

```
_servicename._protocol.domainname. TTL IN SRV priority weight port
target.
```

Let's describe each of the items:

- `servicename` is the name of the given service. For example, `xmpp-client` and `xmpp-server` are two service names that most XMPP servers establish by default. Be sure to maintain the initial underscore character.
- `protocol` is the name of the transport protocol. You are going to need use TCP here, but UDP is another option. Again, be sure to maintain the initial underscore character.
- `domainname` is the domain where the server sits, such as `mcfly.fam`. Notice the period at the end of the domain name field.
- `TTL` is the Time To Live, the longest time that an IP packet can exist for this service. This value is measured in seconds; a value of 86400 is equivalent to 24 hours.
- `IN` is the value for the DNS class field. The value for this field is always `IN`.
- `priority` is the priority of the target host. Lower values take more priority.
- `weight` is used to indicate priority for records that have the same priority. Higher values mean higher preference.
- `port` is the number of the TCP or UDP port that provides the service. For example, this is where `xmpp-client` declares that it uses port 5222, and where `xmpp-server` declares that it uses port 5269.
- `target` is the host name for the machine providing the service. As with the `domainname` field, notice the period at the end of this field.

Let's take a look at the two default SRV records that most XMPP servers establish:

```
_xmpp-client._tcp.example.net. 86400 IN SRV 5 0 5222 example.net.
_xmpp-server._tcp.example.net. 86400 IN SRV 5 0 5269 example.net.
```

This tells us that the `xmpp-client` service uses TCP, sets a TTL of 24 hours, has a priority value of 5 and a weight of 0, and is available on port `5222`. Similarly, `xmpp-service` has the same settings, and will be provided through port `5269`.

You can use the `host`, `dig`, or `nslookup` commands to find existing SRV records.

One thing you can do with SRV records is establish a set of entries that could provide client or server services. This is useful for provisioning your services to provide higher service availability, and to perform load balancing.

Let's look at an example. Suppose we expect a lot of connections to our `xmpp-client` service, so we would like to set up a number of servers that will provide the `xmpp-client` service. We may set up our SRV records in the following way:

```
_xmpp-client._tcp.example.net.  86400  IN SRV 10 70 5222 s1.example.net.
_xmpp-client._tcp.example.net.  86400  IN SRV 10 20 5222 s2.example.net.
_xmpp-client._tcp.example.net.  86400  IN SRV 10 5 5222 s3.example.net.
_xmpp-client._tcp.example.net.  86400  IN SRV 10 5 5222 s4.example.net.
_xmpp-client._tcp.example.net.  86400  IN SRV 15 0 5222 b.example.net.
```

In this example, we have four servers with the same priority. This means the weight field will be used to determine which server will receive the traffic. Notice the weights across all of the servers with priority 10 total to 100 (70 + 20 + 5 + 5); each weight value can be thought of as indicating the percentage of traffic that the server will receive. In this case, `s1.example.net` will receive 70% of the traffic, `s2.example.net` will receive 20%, and so on.

Notice that `b.example.net` has a different priority. A value of 15 indicates a less preferred server, so `b.example.net` (our backup server) will only receive traffic if the more preferred servers are unable to handle it.

# Server-to-server communications

XEP-0288 describes server-to-server connections (S2S), which allows servers to send messages to each other on the same TCP network using bidirectional communication, as opposed to requiring TCP connections between the servers. This allows servers to be connected together and share information seamlessly, and it facilitates the creation of a federated network of servers in which servers can pass along messages to other servers, and clients connected to each server can communicate with clients throughout the entire network. One of the benefits of this behavior is that each server can be set up with its own configuration, modules, components, and users, while also taking advantage of other servers, which have their own configuration.

Prosody supports S2S connections without any work on your part. Let's get started with an example, then we'll work on adding security to this example. First, each server that you wish to connect will need the following lines in `prosody.cfg.lua`:

```
s2s_secure_auth = false // We'll update this soon!
s2s_insecure_domains = { Array of insecure URLs, see below }
```

The module that manages S2S communication (`mod_s2s`) is loaded by default and does not need to appear in your `modules_enabled` list. If you ever want to disable S2S connections on your server, you'll need to add `modules_disabled = { s2s }` to your configuration.

Behind the scenes, the servers send a number of messages to create the connection. You can read all about it in XEP-0288, but suffice to say that the messages will be delivered between servers. For example, suppose you have two servers, `mcfly.fam` and `baines.fam`. You could send a message such as the following:

```
<message from='george@mcfly.fam'
  id='msg-a4f4d8'
  to='lorraine@baines.fam'>
  <body>My density has brought me to you</body>
</message>
```

When George sends this message, the `mcfly.fam` server will receive it and, seeing that it's intended for `baines.fam`, will send it there. The `baines.fam` server will send the message to Lorraine.

Now let's make our federation more secure. If you set `s2s_secure_auth = true` in your configuration, this will configure your server to require encryption and certificate authentication. Other servers will need to provide their certificate; we'll cover certificates in the following section on security.

However, it may be the case that a server you wish to connect to this server simply does not provide certificates that Prosody knows how to trust. You can still connect to such servers when you have `s2s_secure_auth` turned on; this is the role of the `s2s_insecure_domains` setting. Add the name of the domain to that array to allow connections to those servers. For certificate verification to work, you will need to install **LuaSec** version 0.5, or you can get `luasec-prosody` if LuaSec version 0.5 is not available for your operating system. (LuaSec version 0.6 does not work with Prosody.)

Even with `s2s_secure_auth` set to false, you may want to ensure that certain servers are always authenticated. You can use list those servers in another array, `s2s_secure_domains`.

In production you will never want to communicate with insecure domains as this leaves traffic open to reading by third parties. The options should be used purely for development. In 2015 most of the top XMPP service providers (and many much smaller providers) signed up to the XMPP security manifesto which can be found at `https://github.com/stpeter/manifesto`.

# XMPP security

If you are deploying your XMPP server for the world to access, you will want to make sure it is secure! Out of the box, many XMPP servers including Prosody, provide security mechanisms that are easy to set up.

First, let's talk about server certificates. This will be a quick discussion. If you want a secure server, you need to get a server certificate! You can get a certificate from any certificate authority. Recommended authorities are **LetsEncrypt** (`https://letsencrypt.org`) and **StartSSL** (`http://www.startssl.com`), which offer free certificates. In order to use SSL with Prosody you'll need to edit the prosody.cfg.lua file and add the following configuration (pointing to your certificate files):

```
ssl = {
  key = "/path/to/prosody.key";
  certificate = "/path/to/prosody.crt";
}
```

Next, let's talk about encryption. You should ensure that the communication from client to server, and vice versa, is encrypted rather than kept as readable text. All XMPP servers support encryption; Prosody uses OpenSSL for its connection encryption. Let's take a look at the steps necessary to activate encrypted communications. It's very easy. To activate client-to-server encryption on your server side, you will want to use the following line in your `prosody.cfg.lua` file:

```
c2s_require_encryption = true
```

In addition, entering the following line in your `prosody.cfg.lua` file will ensure that plaintext passwords sent over the network are not allowed (although the default value for this setting is false in the first place):

```
allow_unencrypted_plain_auth = false
```

To establish encrypted connection between servers, you will want to use the following line:

```
s2s_require_encryption = true
```

Be sure to restart your server after changing the configuration.

Once you have set up your server certificate and turned encryption on, test the security of your server at the **XMPP IM** Observatory! Visit http://xmpp.net (note: not .org) and enter your public-facing XMPP domain into the **Test a server** field. Select whether you want to test the C2S or S2S connection (remember, these are on different ports), press **Check!**, and see your results!

Server certificates and encryption both facilitate communication security: that is, security with respect to the exchange of information. You will also want to put a high degree of information security in place to ensure that the data on your server is protected from unauthorized access, inspection, or deletion. To ensure information security, you will want to take the following steps:

- Ensure that only authorized users have permission to access files (if you are using file-based storage) or databases that contain XMPP communications and user account information.
- Encrypt the file system that stores your data.
- Install only XMPP components that you trust.
- Activate authentication modules associated with your XMPP server. For example, Prosody provides `mod_auth_internal_hashed`, which stores passwords in hashed form.

# XMPP scalability

When deploying your XMPP capability to the real world, you may need to ensure that your servers will scale. In general, the number of users and JIDs in use at any time has to get pretty high before you need to worry specifically about scalability. Prosody, for example, will handle in the order of hundreds or thousands of users easily. You can find several benchmark test results online and even performance experiments on GitHub that compare the performance of XMPP servers, including Prosody.

As Donald Knuth once said *"Remember that premature optimization is the root of all evil"*. Unless you are experiencing issues due to scalability, you probably do not need to consider the next few paragraphs of advice. Before venturing into the next couple of sections, please be sure that you have cleaned up your server code and you are sure that there is nothing additional that you can squeeze out of the code itself (for example, no duplicated code or functions being called twice, and no loop-invariant operations happening inside a loop).

If you're continuing to read, congratulations! You have a scalability problem to address! Let's take things step by step.

First, recall that we already talked about provisioning services and load balancing under the section on DNS and SRV records. You may want to revisit that section to see how you can employ multiple servers to support your needs.

You may also be interested in clustering. Clustering allows multiple server nodes to service a single domain. At the moment, Prosody does not support clustering (it is slated for the version 1.0 release. At the time of writing, Prosody is at version 0.9.10. If you're interested in watching the ticket for this feature, you can do so at `https://prosody.im/issues/issue/4` `13`). Other XMPP servers, such as ejabberd, do currently support clustering. In ejabberd, it is easy to have a node join or leave a cluster (using the commands `ejabberdctljoin_cluster` and `ejabberdctlleave_cluster`).

Another approach to addressing issues of scalability is to harness the power of asynchronous event notification using `libevent`. Prosody supports `libevent`, which is a library that provides callback functions to a variety of platform monitoring tools such as `kqueue`, `epoll`, and more; it turns out that each operating system (for example, Linux, BSD, or Solaris) has a different function to support nonblocking I/O; libevent provides a layer of abstraction, so you don't have to deal with each of those functions manually. For each operating system, `libevent` will choose the optimal function on the given platform. For more information about `libevent`, see `libevent.org`; there is also an excellent description of how libevent works (and why multi-threading is not the answer!) at `http://www.wangaf` `u.net/~nickm/libevent-book/1_intro.html`.

To enable `libevent` with Prosody, follow these simple steps:

1. Download and install `luaevent`, which provides `libevent` bindings for Lua:

   ```
   sudo apt-get install lua-event
   ```

2. Add the following line to your `prosody.cfg.lua` file (then restart the Prosody server to make the change take hold). You'll probably find this line already entered, but commented out, in your `prosody.cfg.lua` file:

   ```
   use_libevent = true
   ```

Once you restart Prosody, check if Prosody is using the `epoll` or `kqueue` backend. You can check for this in your `prosody.log` file (or whatever name is listed in your `prosody.cfg.lua` file for logging configuration). If it looks like your server is using `select` for connection handling rather than `epoll` or `kqueue`, your request to use `libevent` may not have taken hold.

# User Registration

Earlier in this book, we talked about using the `prosodyctl` command to add users. For example, from the command line, you could enter the following to add a new user (you'll be prompted to enter and retype the password):

```
$ sudo prosodyctl adduser foo@localhost
```

Prosody also provides commands to set the password for a user, or to delete a user (you'll be prompted to enter and retype the password):

```
$ sudo prosodyctl passwd foo@localhost
```

The following command quietly deletes the user:

```
$ sudo prosodyctl deluser foo@localhost
```

Out of the box, Prosody does not provide a command to list the current users for a given host. If you have sufficient permissions, you can list the files in `/var/lib/prosody/{host}/accounts`, where you will see a `.dat` file for each account. But this isn't the right way to do this. Remember `prosody-modules`? It turns out that there is a module for listing users! It's called `mod_listusers`, and if you've followed the steps in the server modules section, you already have a local copy. Place a copy of the Lua file in your modules folder:

```
$ cd /usr/lib/prosody/modules
$ sudo cp ~/prosody-modules/mod_listusers/mod_listusers.lua .
```

Edit your `config` file:

```
$ cd /etc/prosody
$ sudo vi prosody.cfg.lua
```

Add `listusers` to `modules_enabled`, then restart Prosody:

```
$ sudo prosodyctl restart
```

Now you can use the following command to list your users:

```
$ sudo prosodyctl mod_listusers
```

If you happen to be adding several users in a batch process, there is a `prosodyctl` command, register, that lets you do this. If you're interested in batch processing, you might also be interested in migrating a group of users from another server, and you will quickly find tools that support this for Prosody. The `register` command works as follows, but it's a little off-the-books (that is to say, register does not appear when you do `prosodyctl-help`) and `adduser` is the preferred way to add new users:

```
$ sudo prosodyctl <username> <host> <password>
```

So far, we've talked about how you, as the administrator, can add users. There is a way for users to register themselves through an extension, XEP-0077, called **In-Band Registration**. This extension allows any user to add a new user through a set of XMPP messages.

You will need two things for In-Band Registration to work: the `mod_register` module will need to be enabled in `prosody.cfg.lua`, and also, in your `config` file, `allow_registration = true` needs to be set. With In-Band Registration activated on the server, you or an application you write can follow thesesteps to register a user:

1. Send an `iq` request asking for the fields that the host requires to register a user:

```
<iq type="get" id="register" to="mcfly.fam">
    <query xmlns=""jabber:iq:register"" />
</iq>
```

2. The server responds with a result that contains the registration fields. If the server does not support in-band registration, it will return an error, `service-unavailable`. The server might also respond with a redirection, which we'll cover below. Otherwise, the server will respond with an `iq` message such as the following:

```
<iq type="result" id="register">
  <query xmlns="jabber:id:register">
    <instructions>This server requires a username and password
    </instructions>
    <username />
    <password />
  </query>
</iq>
```

The server might also realize that the user who is requesting an account is already registered, based on where the `iq` message is coming from. In that case, it will return an `iq` result that indicates `<registered />`, along with the registration fields completed with the known information (that is, username and password filled in).

3. The client responds with the completed fields:

```
<iq type="set" id="register">
  <query xmlns=""jabber:id:register"">
  <username>martin</username>
  <password>Channels18-24-63-109-87-TWC</password>
</iq>
```

4. The server responds either with success (simply `<iq type="result" id="register">`), or different replies if the user already exists on the server or the registration failed due to incomplete fields. For details on these cases, see the documentation for XEP-0077.

The problem with In-Band Registration is that anyone who can access your server can add new accounts, and these could include spam accounts. The question, then, is how to allow registration while successfully keeping spammers at bay. Fortunately, there are several plugins that can help with this!

Recall in *step 2* that the server might respond with redirection, which permits a different mechanism (generally referred to "Out of Band") to complete the user registration. In this case, the reply from the server will consist only of text in the `instructions` tag, and a URL pointing to the redirected location. For example, the server's reply in *step 2* could have been as follows:

```
<iq type="result" id="register">
    <query xmlns="jabber:iq:register">
        <instructions>To register for an account, please go to
          https://hillvalleycourthouse.mcfly.fam
        </instructions>
        <x xmlns="jabber:x:oob">
            <url>https://hillvalleycourthouse.mcfly.fam</url>
        </x>
    </query>
</iq>
```

In Prosody, you can support registration redirection by installing the `mod_register_redirect` plugin. With the plugin active, you can use the following optional settings in your `prosody.cfg.lua` file to redirect registrants to the right place:

```
registration_whitelist = // array of whitelisted web server IP addresses
registration_url = "https://hillvalleycourthouse.mcfly.fam"
registration_text = "To register for an account, please go to
https://hillvalleycourthouse.mcfly.fam"
registration_oob = true
```

`registration_oob` in the preceding settings and `jabber:x:oob` in the `iq` result refer to the Out-of-Band Data extension, XEP-0066. Basically, you can use **OOB** to specify URLs for transferring information between servers. If your registration is handled not by another server but by some other means (for example, the user needs to complete and e-mail a PDF form to the administrator), then `registration_oob` should be set to false.

There is another plugin, `mod_register_web`, which lets users register for an account using a captcha-protected web form rather than the in-band IQ messages.

# About the XMPP Standards Foundation

The XMPP Standards Foundation (XSF), formerly known as the Jabber Standards Foundation, is a non-profit organization that defines and manages the protocols behind XMPP, including the XMPP Extension Protocols (XEPs, pronounced **"zeps"** partly because they used to be Jabber extensions!), and which provides information and leadership about XMPP to developers, service providers, and users.

The XMPP Council within the XSF is the group that approves XEPs. Members of the council are elected by members of the XSF. Several of the members of the XMPP Council work directly on XMPP libraries, servers (including Prosody!), and other projects.

Individuals may apply to become members of the XSF. Membership is free, and new applicants are admitted based on a vote of the existing members. Even existing members must reapply for membership every year. Those who apply should be able to demonstrate their technical work in supporting the XMPP community through developing code, writing documentation, leading XEPs, and other activities. Members are expected to contribute to the XMPP community and the work performed by the XSF, and are also expected to participate in governance, through voting and attending annual XSF meetings.

While the core XMPP specifications are defined by the Internet Engineering Task Force (IETF), XEPs define extensions to the protocol. New XEPs may have an Experimental status as they are being evaluated; after a successful evaluation, they may be upgraded to Draft status and then, after another round of refinement, to Final, for XEPs on the Standards Track, or Active status for procedural XEPs.

There is a lot of activity happening in the XMPP community, and new XEPs are continually being written and evaluated. The full, up-to-date list of XEPs can be found at `http://xmpp.org/extensions`. Recent XEPs include HTTP and ICE transport methods for Jingle (discussed in the XMPP and WebRTC section), support for OpenPGP, MIX (Multi user chat 2), and considerations for the Internet of Things (also discussed in a later section). To get involved with the XSF, please see `http://xmpp.org`, and get involved via the mailing list and chat rooms.

# XMPP and the new rise of multi-user chat

XMPP is an open standard for federated multi-user communication, with excellent security and well-established user and development communities. There are a lot of commercial services that provide XMPP support and, despite a couple of high-profile departures from the use of XMPP (for example, Google Hangouts and Facebook Chat, which have deprecated their support for XMPP and are using proprietary, walled garden implementations), XMPP represents a solid foundation for building interoperable, multi-user applications.

One great example is **Atlassian HipChat**, which is based on XMPP. And while HipChat competitor Slack does not use XMPP behind the scenes, it does provide an XMPP gateway, which allows you to connect your Jabber client to a Slack server.

Compared to the late 1990, when the Jabber protocol was started and desktops were prevalent, today's most popular devices are mobile. The XSF is actively working on ways to improve XMPP support for mobile deployments (for example, how do we ensure that XMPP makes minimal use of the radio and retains battery life?).

# XMPP and the Internet of Things

The Internet of Things (IoT) enables the connection of devices of all sorts and describes how they communicate data with each other and with servers, and XMPP is at the forefront of this growing area. With years of experience in security and scalability, as well as the existence of a plethora of servers and related software, XMPP provides a solid and open foundation for the infrastructure of IoT. There are several XEPs to support XMPP's role in IoT, and there is a specific community, called XMPP-IoT, which focuses on this initiative (see `http://www.xmpp-iot.org`).

IoT communications are commonly thought of as Device-To-Device (D2D) and Device-To-Server (D2S); it is useful to keep these different levels of communication in mind as you explore IoT and notice the range of protocols being developed to support these use cases. XMPP is preferred in the D2S space; the D2D space often involves protocols that are a bit closer to the wire and which, perhaps, do not rely on the TCP transport layer.

There are several experimental XEPs that support XMPP-IoT, as shown in the following table. (Experimental means the XEP is not yet a draft and has not yet been approved by the XSF, but exploratory implementation in new code is encouraged.):

| XEP-0323 | Internet of Things – Sensor Data | **Provides the common framework for sensor data interchange over XMPP networks** |
| --- | --- | --- |
| XEP-0324 | Internet of Things – Provisioning | Describes an architecture for efficient provisioning of services, access rights, and user privileges for the Internet of Things, where communication between Things is done using the XMPP protocol |
| XEP-0325 | Internet of Things – Control | Describes how to control devices or actuators in an XMPP-based sensor network |
| XEP-0326 | Internet of Things – Concentrators | Describes how to manage and get information from concentrators of devices over XMPP networks |
| XEP-0347 | Internet of Things – Discovery | Describes an architecture based on the XMPP protocol, whereby Things can be installed and safely discovered by their owners and connected into networks of Things |

XEPs for the Internet of Things

In addition to these XEPs that have the phrase Internet of Things in their title, there are several other extension protocols that these depend on that are not necessarily specific to IoT. For example, XEP-0322 describes the use of the Efficient XML Interchange (EXI) format, which can be used generally in XMPP communications, and may be specifically useful in IoT communications. There are likely to be additional XEPs related to IoT in the future. If you are interested in IoT, this is an excellent time to get involved in the development of standards and applications that will push the envelope on future capabilities.

For much more detail on XMPP and the Internet of Things, please see *Learning Internet of Things* by *Peter Waher*.

# XMPP and Universal Plug-n-Play

Universal Plug-n-Play (UPnP) is a protocol standard that lets devices, such as computers, printers and other peripherals, and mobile and wireless devices, discover the presence and functionality of other devices on a network. It uses TCP/IP and HTTP to let devices perform discovery and data transfer. The UPnP standard is managed by the Open Connectivity Foundation (`http://openconnectivity.org`), and it is another protocol in the Internet of Things space.

There is an extension to UPnP called **UPnP Cloud Annex (UCA)**, which is based on XMPP and binds open standards XMPP messages to UPnP protocols. The XSF has the UPnP Liaison Team, which is responsible for ensuring that the development of UPnP and the use of XMPP within the UPnP community is consistent with XMPP standards.

As with the Internet of Things, you can find more information about UPnP in *Learning Internet of Things* by *Peter Waher*. UPnP is under very active development, and you will also find up-to-date information and spec status at http://openconnectivity.org.

# XMPP and WebRTC

**Web Real-Time Communication** (WebRTC) is an open-standard project from the World Wide Web Consortium (W3C), which lets browsers and applications share real-time communication (for example, voice and video calls) using a set of simple APIs. WebRTC is a Peer-To-Peer (P2P) protocol (meaning there is no need for a server!), and it does not specify a protocol for signaling between peers.

Jingle, described in XEP-0166 and XEP-0167, is an XMPP extension that lets P2P clients share audio and video data. It facilitates applications such as Voice over IP (VoIP) and video conferencing, and it can serve as the signaling initiation protocol for WebRTC applications.

Google has developed a library called libjingle that can be used to create P2P connections and exchange data in multi-user applications. Interestingly, libjingle and the XSF's Jingle standard are similar but not interoperable, since both were created in parallel at approximately the same time. You can read more at https://developers.google.com/talk/libjingle/developer_guide. On this page, Google does indicate their intention to implement the official Jingle XEP.

Several clients, including Empathy, provide support for Jingle, and provide VoIP and videoconferencing capabilities. Since Jingle is P2P, there is no need for servers (such as Prosody) to provide support for the XEP, since it is purely a client-based capability. However, when a server is involved in passing messages to its clients, improperly formatted messages may be rejected by a server. **Jitsi** (http://www.jitsi.org) is a great example of another client that supports XMPP and Jingle.

# The Future of XMPP

As evidenced by the new XEPs and applications of XMPP in new and emerging application areas, it is clear that XMPP has a bright future. You can be a part of that future by developing applications that use XMPP, as well as by contributing XEPs to cover new areas as yet unexplored. In fact, XEP-0143, Guidelines for Authors of XMPP Extension Protocols, speaks directly about things to keep in mind as you suggest ideas for the continuing growth of the protocol.

XEP-0143 is clear about the technical work necessary to submit a new extension. We'd also like to touch on some non-technical aspects that are just as important as a technically sound proposal. During the XSF's review of the XEP and even after the XSF Council moves your XEP to the Final state, if it is accepted, it's especially important that you continue to communicate and be an advocate for your protocol. The mere existence of an extension does not mean that people will immediately flock to it; rather, you must get the message out! You'll need to let people know about your extension, document it with clear examples and code, communicate the benefits, and help people easily understand what it can do and how it differs from other work in other protocols. In essence, you need to become the developer evangelist for your new creation. No one else is better suited for the role than you.

We encourage you to be the engineer that is empowered to do what they need to do to advocate for your cause and your work, and make the change you want to see in the world. The role of an engineer is to improve the quality of life for humanity. Your XMPP contributions are one important step in the big picture, and for the future of XMPP.

# Summary

In this chapter, we have introduced several important XMPP extension protocols (XEPs) that enable the functionality necessary to deploy real-world XMPP applications. These extensions and capabilities include server modules, DNS setup and SRV records, server-to-server communications, security, and scalability.

We have also introduced you to the XMPP Standards Foundation (XSF) and provided an overview of how XMPP supports new capabilities, such as advancements in multi-user chat, the Internet of Things (IoT), Universal Plug and Play (UPnP), and Web Real-Time Communication (WebRTC).

We have also encouraged you to participate in the XMPP community to help address emerging needs, in the process benefitting all users of this open protocol. Finally, we wish you all the best as you develop your XMPP-based applications!

# Index